MW01075773

"Kipp's passion, experience, joy, ar
points us to a future in youth minist
on practical wisdom for longevity an
to use this book in youth ministry classes."

Wendy Mohler-Seib
Director of Faith Formation
Institute for Discipleship, Southwestern College

"Kipp has produced a youth ministry text that is contemporary in understanding the challenges youth ministers will face in today's world. *Making Room* is well supported with Scripture and current research, and comprehensively addresses both what it means to be a youth minister as well as what an effective youth minister needs to know and do. This is a book I will adopt for my course on youth ministry!"

Jana Sundene
Associate Professor of Christian Ministries
Trinity International University

"*Making Room* is a practically relevant and theologically rich guide for young youth ministers seeking to understand the journey before them. Kipp recognizes that youth and youth ministry have shifted significantly over the years. Addressing this shift, Kipp invites the reader to look over his shoulder as he brings his own ministerial experience to bear on current theological and developmental realities. What makes this treatment unique is the invitation to hear from other scholars and practitioners throughout the narrative. The placement of these voices adds depth and diversity to the presentation of the material. I agree with Kipp that we need a larger, more intentional vision of youth ministry. Making Room accomplishes this and more, providing a unique and worthy addition to the conversation. I wholeheartedly recommend this book."

Steven Bonner
Assistant Dean of Undergraduate Bible
Associate Professor of Christian Ministry
Lipscomb University

"*Making Room* is incredibly helpful for those who are starting in youth ministry and for those who are interested in doing youth ministry in a transformative way. This well-researched, insightful, and practical book is sure to help both churches and youth leaders create youth ministries that are integrated into the life of the church for the long haul, which is when and where true transformation happens."

Brian Hull
Associate Professor of Youth Ministry
Asbury University

"*Making Room* is a powerful book thoughtfully written with practical and insightful steps for creating a flourishing ministry with youth. Kipp delves deeply into the body and mission of Christ to inform a concept of youth ministry that stands the test of time and cultural change. Then he extrapolates that solid theology into an incredible vision to transform generations of youth with the power of the gospel. I encourage every youth worker to read this book and then pass it along to the generations we hope will follow in the faith and in ministry."

Dave Curtiss
USA Director
The Great Commission Foundation

MAKING

ROOM

The Purpose and Practice of Youth Ministry

Michael A. Kipp

THE FOUNDRY
PUBLISHING

Copyright © 2021 by Michael A. Kipp
The Foundry Publishing®
PO Box 419527
Kansas City, MO 64141
thefoundrypublishing.com

978-0-8341-3930-5

Printed in the
United States of America

Cover design: J.R. Caines
Interior Design: Sharon Page

Library of Congress Cataloging-in-Publication Data
A complete catalog record for this book is available from the Library of Congress.

The Internet addresses, email addresses, and phone numbers in this book are accurate at the time of publication. They are provided as a resource. The Foundry Publishing does not endorse them or vouch for their content or permanence.

10 9 8 7 6 5 4 3 2 1

*To the many past, current, and future youth workers
and pastors with whom I've had (and will have) the privilege
to serve. May we all seek to lead God's children
into deeper relationship with Christ's church
and Christ's mission.*

Contents

• • • • • • • • • • • • • •

Acknowledgments
9

Preface
11

Introduction
15

Section I: Beginning Things
1. Beginning with the End in Mind: Integrating Young People
into the Body of Christ and the Mission of Christ
25

2. Falling Forward: Transitioning to a Ministry That Integrates
Young People into the Body of Christ and into the Mission of Christ
by Johnny Hampton
39

Section II: Integration Starts with You!: Toward Health, Longevity, and Structure
3. Exegeting the Community: The Importance of Integration
with Pastor and Community
57

Section III: Adolescent Development and Spiritual Commitment
4. Adolescent Development and Spiritual Formation
by Mindy Coates Smith
87

5. Taking the Next Faithful Step: What Does This Look Like?
95

Section IV: Becoming a Practical Ecclesiologist, or What Does This Look Like in Real Life?
6. Making Room
103

Section V: Toward a Transforming Vision of Ministry for Self, Others, and the Church

7. It *All* Starts with You . . . Surprise!
129

8. The *Imago Dei* and Missional Ministry to Youth
by Tom Combes
152

Excursus: How Did We Get Here? A Brief History of Christian Education and the Emergence of Youth Ministry
by Mark A. Maddix
163

Appendix A: Sunday School Exchange #1
183

Appendix B: Sunday School Exchange #2
185

Bibliography
187

Notes
197

Acknowledgments

· · · · · · · · · · · ·

ALTHOUGH IT IS IMPOSSIBLE to list all the many folks who've been so kind along this journey and contributed to my own formation in the faith and ministry, I will list a few who stand out: Bill Hackler, Inter-Varsity (UCSB), Trent Buckle, Brennan Manning, Dave Curtiss, Mike Ford, Jason Beagle, SonShine Ministries, John Payton, Mark and Janet Haidet, Dave Smee, Rob and Tracy Kitzman (and so many other incredible volunteer youth workers at SLONAZ! . . . and the young people who taught me how to be a pastor there), Ed Robinson, Kenda Creasy Dean, Aisling Zweigle, Stephen Elliott, Brent and Lori Kall, Brian and Carol Hull, Jesse Middendorf, Daniel Ketchum, Kenny Wade, Nikki Schmidt, Eric Schmidt, Eunice Smith, Keegan Lenker, Joel Pearsall, Daryl Johnson, Johnny Hampton, Melissa (Davis) Teeter, Zach Schulz, College Church of the Nazarene in Nampa, Idaho, Ralph Neill, Mark Maddix, Brent Peterson and my colleagues and students in the School of Theology and Christian Ministry at Northwest Nazarene University, Chap Clark, Ray S. Anderson, my pastor T. Scott Daniels, and my College Church ministry colleagues (past and present): Tharon, Rich, Heather, Ryan, Ashley, Jess, Ali, Chelsea, Drew, Heather, Bree, Coltin, Erika, and Natalie.

To my kids—Spencer and McKenna—I never knew my heart could love this way until you were born.

Finally, to the one whom my soul loves: Sandy. I can't imagine a better adventure partner than you!

Preface

• • • • • • • • • • • •

IN DECEMBER 1990 I was recruited to be a junior high school volunteer youth worker. I was having a great time at a college Christmas party and a friend said something like, "Hey, you should work with junior highers at our church."

I said something like, "Really? Sounds fun."

And that was my beginning in youth ministry.

I was not a model volunteer. Although I followed Jesus with as much of my whole self as I understood at age twenty, I didn't really understand my role as a volunteer working with youth. That was obvious by my lack of preparation, infrequent prayer for the young people I worked with, and frequent absences from youth group and volunteer staff meetings. Two years later when the outgoing youth pastor recommended me to replace him, I was flabbergasted.

However, 1 Corinthians 1:27–29 (ESV) reminds us, "God chose the foolish things of the world to shame the wise; God chose the weak things of the world to shame the strong. God chose the lowly things of this world and the despised things—and the things that are not—to nullify the things that are, so that no one may boast before him."

I certainly fit the description of "foolish," "weak," "lowly," and "not."

God was in this "call" and made that clear to me. And so, with a humble, contrite, and terrified heart I accepted the call to be the youth pastor. Well, to be honest, I was initially the "interim summer senior high youth intern." Really! The church was obviously not so sure about me! They interviewed a lot of other candidates to be the full-time youth pastor, but none worked out, so finally they offered the job to me.

The next thirty months were great, lonely, fulfilling, difficult, challenging, joy-filled, and heartbreaking. I was smart enough to not change the program much. The previous youth pastor had been brilliant and beloved. I followed his lead and learned a great deal by doing so. I had some of the most dedicated and astute youth volunteers I have ever encountered. But about two years in, I realized that, although I was a good manager, I did not have the chops to be a good pastor. I didn't know enough about the Bible, theology, church history, pastoral care, church politics, psychology, adolescent development, family systems, and more to do this for the long haul, which I believed God intended for me to do.

I spoke with God about this repeatedly until I realized the answer was for me to attend seminary. So in January of 1996, I set off for our denomination's theological seminary in Kansas City. The experience was transformative. I do not know where I would be today if it were not for that place, those people, and that time.

I was privileged to work throughout my seminary experience with that same brilliant and beloved youth pastor I had followed in my previous church. Those years of the combined experience of the back-and-forth nature between the academy and the local church were deeply formative. I spent fewer than three years in Kansas City but gained at least twice that amount in youth ministry experience through the relationships with strong, capable mentors in both the church and the academy.

In 1998, I came to Nampa, Idaho, to be the pastor to students and their families at College Church of the Nazarene. I struggled with how to pastor families well. In a small way, taking on that title birthed in me a quest to learn how to better connect not only with youth but also with their families and entire support systems. I had no concrete idea how to do that with excellence.

Almost from the beginning of that role in Nampa, I was invited to serve as an adjunct at Northwest Nazarene University (NNU). The prospect of teaching college students about youth ministry terrified me. Did I have enough to say? What if they were smarter than I was? I invited two good youth worker friends to join me in this new enterprise. For the next five years, we taught the youth ministry course at NNU together.

We collaborated on a syllabus, chose texts, and created a curriculum for the one course that youth ministry minors would take at the university. This forced us all to think deeply about the essential focus of youth ministry. It was intimidating to consider that what we decided was "vital" youth ministry knowledge would shape young, budding youth workers. We took the challenge seriously and drew upon the best resources and ideas we had encountered. We sought to creatively shape the course, our assignments. and projects. We even took the students on field trips to observe how youth culture had evolved, even since they were high school students.

During our fifth year, I was asked to teach a second class. Shortly thereafter I was invited to apply for the position of professor of youth and family ministry at NNU. While restructuring the School of Theology and Christian Ministry, the university created a new position to give proper attention to the large number of students coming to study youth ministry. Again, I was intimidated, but sensed God in the middle of this and applied.

When I was offered the job, I was again flabbergasted. They assured me that they saw something in me and sensed a great fit with what I was doing, who I was, and the role they envisioned for this position. They also informed me that accepting the position meant I needed to enroll in a doctoral program. The following January, I began doctoral work at Fuller Theological Seminary.

That was 2004. Since then, I've come to understand my position to act not only as a teacher to students at NNU but also as a resource to my church, my denomination, youth ministry as a vocation, and Christ's church. It is a high and humbling venture and one I take seriously. I've learned that I must do the reading, reflecting, and writing to help my colleagues in local churches sharpen their focus in youth ministry. I've come to understand common, shortsighted patterns youth workers get caught in and to sense that part of my role is to point these out and correct them.

Teaching youth ministry causes a person to closely examine their own practice and outcomes. In my case, these were not always favorable or perhaps even Christian. I am a brother who has made many mistakes and hopes to transparently confess them and offer corrections to others in this generation of youth ministers. This is a book for practitioners—paid, volunteer, part-time, full-time, bivocational, young, old, and in any denomination. Simultaneously, I believe it will be useful in the academic classroom. I would ask the reader to remember that it is written from the heart of someone who loves young people and wants to help youth workers consider how best to shape our ministries in ways that demonstrate a vital connection to the body of Christ as critical to live the very best life available. I write from my tradition—Wesleyan, and specifically the Church of the Nazarene—but hope this work will translate easily to any tradition, polity, structure, or setting.

Enter this project. Long gone is the day of simply having fun with young people and building relationships in the name of Jesus and youth ministry. It is not enough—perhaps it has never been—to simply provide alternative activities and subculture for young people to "keep them out of trouble." We clearly need a larger, more intentional vision of youth ministry in the body of Christ. And the focus of this discussion will center on integrating young people into the body of Christ and the mission of Christ. This represents a new look at a very, very old vision . . . the vision we should have always had in the practice of youth ministry.

Introduction

• • • • • • • • • • • • •

I HAVE A GROWING CONVICTION that we practitioners of youth ministry do not seem to change with the times. So much that is fundamental to the youth ministry movement has profoundly altered, and yet corresponding changes to the practice of youth ministry have not seemed to happen.

To begin, the culture around us has shifted. Once the Bible had great authority in our culture, and pastors were highly respected leaders in the community. Then the test of "truth" became all about empirical data. The Enlightenment ultimately ushered in the scientific method and began the reign of human reason. "Truth" had to be measured, observed, verified, and quantified.

Today the lines are changing once again and almost anything can be accepted as "true" depending upon the speaker, hearer, and the community in which they are embedded. Both science and faith have become suspect (although science less so). It seems many of our friends, neighbors, and coworkers are, sadly, much more open to any religious system besides Christianity.

A second shift in society regards the common person's view of the church. At one time the Christian church had a solid reputation and was known as an institution that cared for the poor, broken, downtrodden, and the lonely. That reputation has been battered in the ensuing years—much due to self-inflicted stupidity and selfishness.

Today we have entered a time of being post-Christian. No longer does the average person have a basic knowledge of the primary tenets of Christianity or the Bible or respect for a person of the cloth.

Another example is how families have changed. In 1970, "no fault" divorce began in California and soon swept the country. The proponents of this new law believed that streamlining the divorce process would be good for marriage and families because people who did not want to be married or were stuck in a bad or abusive marriage would be able to remedy their situation more easily. The proponents believed that dissolving bad marriages would, overall, strengthen marriage in our country.

Instead, the opposite has occurred as the divorce rate has soared to nearly one in two marriages ending in divorce. This legislation left in its wake a mass of broken families—men, women, and children.

This is only one aspect of the change in marriage and families. Another tectonic shift was brought by the marriage equality act, which legalized the marriage of same-sex couples. Since 2015, this law of the land has already initiated quantum shifts in what it means to be "family."

As if this weren't enough, the entire period and understanding of adolescence has been transformed. At the turn of the twentieth century, the entire period of adolescence lasted about one and a half years.[1] That means from puberty to finding one's place in the world was completed in an average of eighteen months.

Today that figure has increased nearly tenfold. Now young people enter adolescence (puberty) at about eleven years of age and find their place in the world in their late twenties. (Many twenty-somethings argue that thirty is the mark of adulthood.[2]) In just over one hundred years—a few generations—what it means to be a "young person" has radically changed.

Lots of changes have occurred all around and even *in* the period of adolescence—the culture, the church, families, and the institution of marriage—even the period of life most youth ministry focuses on. Yet here's the staggering news in the middle of this change: The practice of youth ministry has remained basically the same since the 1950s (crowd breaker, a few songs, a skit, and devotion . . . and see you next week). Could this be part of the reason why forty to fifty percent of all high school graduates leave the church?[3] Maybe we are seeking to minister in a way that simply does not fit the times or the reality of our situation.

What to Do

Telos is a concept central to this entire shift and the needed corrective. This term is often discussed in undergraduate philosophy courses in connection with Aristotle. Aristotle referenced two different ways of viewing an action. First, *poiesis*. This is best understood as "an action that produces a result," such as a watchmaker building a watch or a carpenter building a desk.[4] The result of the worker's action is a product, a watch, or a desk.

This way of looking at an action includes no concern to the future use of the watch by the watchmaker or the desk by the carpenter. The watchmaker does not care whether the watch is used to keep time in France, Germany, or Antarctica, or by a man, woman, child, or machine. The maker is not concerned if the watch is used for sinister purposes, such as a timing mechanism in an explosive device.

Similarly, the carpenter gives no real thought to the future use of the desk. It may provide the surface for a child doing nightly homework, a mother changing her child's diaper, or an elderly man writing checks to pay his bills. Each worker set out to fashion a product and has done so. The completion of the product completes the action.

Are you with me so far?

The second way Aristotle viewed an action is that of *praxis*.[5] An important distinction between *praxis* and *poiesis* involves the notion of *telos* or the future "use or purpose."[6] To say it differently, an action that is characteristic of *praxis,* as opposed to that of *poiesis,* is designed with a specific end in mind.

Ray S. Anderson, the long-time and brilliant professor of practical theology at Fuller Theological Seminary, goes even further to say that in *praxis*, "the action not only produces a product but the action is accountable to the *telos* and, in moving toward the *telos*, is informed by the *telos* as to the kind of action required in order to produce the intended effect."[7]

The praxis involves seeking to create something, and in the very act of creation is accountable to the use or purpose of that item. Due to that accountability, the creator pays close attention to the creation's outcome to ensure that the item is designed to fulfill the purpose for which it was created. The very act of creation is reflexive and the creator cares deeply about the way a thing is used.

Going back to the watchmaker—in *praxis*, the watchmaker produces the watch in a way that ensures it could never be used for timing in an explosive device. Because the watchmaker's action is accountable to the final product, they design that final product to keep perfect time but not to be used for evil purposes.

In describing this kind of action in the context of the practice of ministry Anderson forces us to consider our role as ministers of the gospel. Exactly what are we setting out to do? If we are going to be involved in a ministry of *praxis*, we must know and define what that purpose or goal is from the beginning. In fact, Anderson tells us that the purpose or goal we have in mind will inform the way we act and will also cause us to do things differently along the way to keep in line with that goal.

So, what is the *telos* of youth ministry? What exactly do we hope to accomplish? What is the goal or aim? Muse on that for a moment.

In Matthew 5:48, we read an often-misunderstood directive of Jesus in the Sermon on the Mount as he states, "Be perfect, therefore, as your heavenly Father is perfect."

The word translated as "perfect" is actually the Greek word *telos*. The word can also connote "completeness," and being "whole" or "total."[8]

The command on the lips of Jesus references Leviticus 19:2 where Israel is called to, "Be holy because I, the LORD your God, am holy."

The context for each of these commands is about living in harmony with the law. In the Old Testament this would have meant Mosaic Law, but from Jesus, this refers to the new covenant "law" of love—a love that is even extended to a person's enemies and is characterized by "volitional acts for the benefit and well-being of others," not simply by emotions or feelings.[9]

Those from the Wesleyan tradition see the fulfillment or *telos* of Jesus's command here, in Matthew 5:48, in a heart of love for God, humanity, and even all of creation. We understand that to love is the highest calling of being human, for it is the primary way we understand God's character as a God of love. Rather than "not sinning" or attaining some objective standard of absolute "perfection," meaning without blemish or fault, we see love as the fulfillment of the law as God intended it.[10]

So, the *telos* here is to connect why humanity exists with the purpose of the practice of youth ministry. Humans exist to receive and give love to God and each other, and the practice of youth ministry seeks to capitalize on that love through relationally integrating young people into the body of Christ and the mission of Christ.

In his great book *The Ministry of Nurture*, Duffy Robbins stated, "The purpose of youth ministry is to help teenagers grow spiritually."[11] I argue that this simply is not enough. It's not enough to only foster spiritual growth. That is a good and important goal, but if that is the end for the entire pursuit of ministry to and with young people, it is anemic. I'm arguing for a higher end goal (and frankly, what I believe Robbins meant). The discernable difference in the practice of this genus of youth ministry is always on the objective outcome of those six or seven years of working with early and middle adolescents as becoming faithful followers of Christ and participants in his body and mission. (And by the way, a person cannot become a "faithful follower of Christ" and not participate in his body and mission as well.) And yet, much of the contemporary practice of youth ministry appears to ignore this truth by separating young people from the rest of the faith community for much of their adolescent years. I do believe young people should have time in age-appropriate Christian formation, but they also need regular time spent with the intergenerational body of Christ. If either of these is out of balance, there is not a sense of wholeness or completeness. It seems we have erred for too long on the side of segregation by age.

This type of youth ministry practice is categorically different from other noble, yet shortsighted, goals of maintaining sexual purity, remaining drug and alcohol free, being "good kids," and even personal salvation.

Yes, I said it. Something is more important than persuading (or even manipulating) a young person into saying a prayer, even the Sinner's Prayer. After all, what good is that prayer if nothing comes of it? What have we really done if a young person genuinely repents of sin and seeks forgiveness from God, if they are not intentionally connected to the body of Christ? What has really been done if we have not helped youth begin to form a vision for their lives that is big enough to sustain their interest, passion, and commitment such as that of being a part of the mission of Christ?

The primary issue at stake here is that of orbit. What does the orbit of young people include after youth group? Likely it includes work, school, social media, and relationships, but does it include Christianity? The church? Corporate worship? Does a young person have any part of their life after youth group that would distinguish that they are a follower of Jesus?

If not, then perhaps youth group did not successfully fulfill its purpose. Of course, a *lot* of other factors are involved in a young person's spiritual formation and connection to the body of Christ, such as the family and parents' connection. But should we be asking how the youth ministry has contributed to that and how it has sought to invite parents and families into the fold?

Another way to say it is: The goal is to help establish certain practices and rhythms in young peoples' lives. You've probably heard the saying, "You are what you eat." Philosopher Jamie Smith suggests, "You are what you love" and we demonstrate our "loves" through our habits and what we give ourselves to—in short, our practices.[12]

The practices and rhythms of the follower of Jesus would include intergenerational fellowship with other believers, Bible study, attending to the sacraments, silence, solitude, fasting, corporate worship, and life-giving service to others, to name a few practices. How are we doing in those areas? What kind of patterns of "orbit" are we systemically helping the young people in our ministries to establish? Are we simply providing Christian entertainment for a few years, or are we meaningfully integrating them into the body of Christ and giving them a vision for life that aligns with the mission of the holy and resurrected One?

Perhaps the best way to communicate my thought is to share this blog post a former youth group participant, Kevin, wrote several years ago:

> I attended the church next to our college campus. The youth ministry was incredible. We went on mission trips to Mexico and discipleship retreats to monasteries. We regularly had intensive spiritual formation retreats that involved fasting, studying Scripture, serving the poor, prayer labyrinths, and the like. My youth group had Ash Wednesday services and Holy Week services.
>
> On top of that, I was a very nerdy Bible quizzer, which more than any biblical or spiritual benefit, connected me to the other churches on our district and gave me some of the best friends I have ever had.
>
> During my senior year of high school, the children's pastor arranged with my youth pastor for me to teach four-year-olds in Sunday school, which led to future leadership in the children's ministry. . . . When I went to seminary, I became aware that my youth group experience was unique. . . . I realized that while I was

fasting for Holy Week, other teens were hiding Easter eggs. While I was spending twenty-four hours in silence at a monastery, other youth group kids were bowling. While I was memorizing John to compete at Bible quizzing, others were watching *VeggieTales*. . . . A few things make my story unique from others' stories. The first is that through Bible quizzing and an incredible youth group experience . . . I had very strong ties to the church. I do not believe that is the norm. In fact, most evangelical youth ministries are incredibly shallow.

Second, I was involved in congregational leadership (albeit very minor) when I graduated from high school. Note that was *not* youth group leadership. It was a position in another ministry in the church.[13]

Kevin's experience demonstrates attempts to shift the orbit from entertainment to meaningful encounter to service to spiritual disciplines and, though implicit, connection to adults beyond youth group volunteers. It also reveals a consistent connection to the Christian calendar and the accompanying rhythm of reflection on the human condition that comes through these times of celebration and fasting that are part of walking through the church year. Moving beyond the entertainment model to a more reflective model enables young people to consider for what and, more importantly, for whom they are living. These considerations come when times of silence, fasting, and walking prayer paths are woven into the fabric of a young person's youth group experience. Thankfully, these provided "sticking points" for Kevin in his faith journey. They were enough to keep him connected to the body of Christ in college and beyond. Today Kevin pastors a church and hopes to do the same sorts of things that helped him to develop a vision for his life.

SECTION I
BEGINNING THINGS

Beginning with the End in Mind
Integrating Young People into the Body of Christ and the Mission of Christ

● ● ● ● ● ● ● ● ● ● ● ● ●

IT IS IMPERATIVE to have a firm grasp on this goal of "integrating young people into the body of Christ and the mission of Christ." Let's look at each of the four parts of this purpose individually.

#1—"Integrating"

The act of integration is the "incorporation as equals into . . . an organization of individuals of different groups" or "the combining and coordinating of separate parts or elements into a unified whole."[1] Think about how very different these two definitions look compared to what has typically been accepted in youth ministry. The different age groups in the church to be *equal* and *combined* in a *unified whole*, is the idea here. No longer does one group see another as less or more, but each sees the other as vital to the health of the whole body.

In commenting on the reality of youth group kids leaving the church after high school, Sharon Galgay Ketcham argues, "In reality, there is not actually a retention problem. That would mean youth were connected to the faith community and then left. Instead, there is an integration problem. Youth ministries, broadly speaking, do not appear to be helping youth become part of the community of faith."[2]

Paul's words from 1 Corinthians 12:12–26 come to mind:

For just as the body is one and has many members, and all the members of the body, though many, are one body, so it is with Christ. For in the one Spirit we were all baptized into one body—Jews or Greeks, slaves or free—and we were all made to drink of one Spirit.

Indeed, the body does not consist of one member but of many. If the foot would say, "Because I am not a hand, I do not belong to the body," that would not make it any less a part of the body. And if the ear would say, "Because I am not an eye, I do not belong to the body," that would not make it any less a part of the body. If the whole body were an eye, where would the hearing be? If the whole body were hearing, where would the sense of smell be? But as it is, God arranged the members in the body, each one of them, as he chose. If all were a single member, where would the body be? As it is, there are many members, yet one body. The eye cannot say to the hand, "I have no need of you," nor again the head to the feet, "I have no need of you." On the contrary, the members of the body that seem to be weaker are indispensable, and those members of the body that we think less honorable we clothe with greater honor, and our less respectable members are treated with greater respect; whereas our more respectable members do not need this. But God has so arranged the body, giving the greater honor to the inferior member, that there may be no dissension within the body, but the members may have the same care for one another. If one member suffers, all suffer together with it; if one member is honored, all rejoice together with it. (NRSV)

In this central passage regarding unity and even *integration*, the apostle Paul argues for the importance of each part of the body. Paul's strong statement of the many parts of the body being necessary to form the body being as "it is with Christ" (v. 12) leads us to draw some provocative conclusions about the church and the current practice of youth ministry. It does not seem a stretch to see the youth of the church as feeling like feet and ears[3] against that of hands and eyes (vv. 15–16). Often the young are treated as if the other, older parts do not need them (v. 21).[4] The young, perhaps like other marginalized populations, are often denied positions of leadership and meaningful roles of ministry within the church. And this, it seems, is the "natural order of things"[5] in our world.

However, the body of Christ should not function according to the natural order of things. Instead, "the members of the body that seem to be weaker are indispensable, and those members of the body that we think less honorable we clothe with greater honor, and our less respectable members are treated with greater respect" (vv. 22–23, NRSV).

Paul argued for us not simply to provide a "space" for the weaker parts, but to give them a voice in the body. For "if one member suffers, all suffer together with it" (v. 26, NRSV). How then can we marginalize, segregate, and dishonor any single part of the body? This is what occurs when young people are separated from the body and treated as vestigial organs rather than full, participating members of the body.[6]

Paul clearly demonstrated that when the body is separated into its constituent parts, it will not survive. All parts functioning together are necessary to the body's health. Where is the "interdependence" of the various parts? Perhaps a more appropriate and biblical approach to youth ministry might look like Figure 1 (below). In this diagram, the youth ministry is a subset within the local expression of the body of Christ. Further, it has a permeable boundary, which illustrates the nature of being a distinct group within the body but interdependent, not independent. This allows for diversity but demonstrates the necessity of the interaction with the greater community of faith. Further, this organization fosters interdependence as each part of the body utilizes its unique gifts for the common good of the whole and, by definition, enables the body to thrive through the interaction and a natural feedback that is created. This interdependence, interaction, and ensuing feedback serves as the "nerve network" throughout the body that monitors overall health and well-being, which cannot otherwise be maintained.

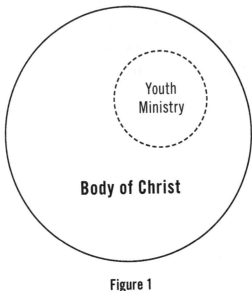

Figure 1

#2—"Young People . . ."

In a 2008 issue of *Youth Worker Journal,* Christian Smith wrote a piece[7] pleading with youth workers to stop calling young people "students," noting that whether due to dropping out or some other unfortunate situation, not all young people are students.

Perhaps because my twenty-eight years in youth ministry have been in relatively affluent churches and their accompanying communities, this never occurred to me. And now as a professor, I was still using it. I always had. Bad form. Now I was convicted.

More importantly, however, is the functional bias the term "student" reveals. First it seems to locate youth ministry in a socioeconomic class (i.e., middle and upper) where a young person is more likely to be a student. Does that mean that lower socioeconomic populations should not be the focus of youth ministry efforts? Of course not, but a person could construe it this way, though that is not intended. Our language matters a great deal.

However, most important to this discussion is the way the term "student" objectifies a human by using a label to describe what they do, not who they are. We are our relationships—not our functions.[8] Labeling like this makes objects of people and destroys the potential for relationship. Andy Root commented, "A person is infinitely more than any functional definition. To go with *student* in student ministry is to wade into the murky waters of individualism."[9] Root writes lucidly about the importance of the interrelationship of Father, Son, and Spirit and how these relationships give form to all human relationships. Our relationship of person to person, son to father, mother to daughter, spouse to spouse, and friend to friend define our being. "People are their relationships."[10]

Conversely the instrumental, functional definitions of teacher, mail carrier, scientist, manager, plumber, and so forth only objectify one another. Although useful to some degree in understanding what a person does for a living or the function they serve in the world, it does not get at *who* they are. We best understand who a person is as the totality of their relationships.

To this end, Smith, Root, and I submit that we should not call our youth "students" but rather children, youth, adolescents, kids, teens (maybe), or young people. After all, that is who they are in relationship with the other people of Christ's body.

#3—"Into the Body of Christ . . ."

To be clear, when we talk of the "body" of Christ we refer to the crucified physical body of the Lord Jesus. Before his crucifixion Jesus translated this event for the disciples at the Last Supper (Matthew 26, Mark 14, Luke 22, and John 6). So now, as we speak of the body of Christ, this reference calls to mind the sacrament of Communion or the Eucharist. This same crucified body is how the new, mystical body of Christ is formed—through baptism into Christ, we are now all one body.[11] In 1 Corinthians 12 (referenced previously), Paul illustrates the very different nature of this Christ-initiated, human organization.

Simply put, the enduring nature of the body of Christ—the church—is reason enough to want to meaningfully integrate young people into it. Its enduring quality ensures an unending resource of love, relationship, and support. This cannot be overstated in a world where so much is temporary—particularly relationships. The church stands as a beacon of long-lasting hospitality, belonging, and personal connection. This is the kind of association a young person needs.

The significant report *Hardwired to Connect* gives a clarion call for such enduring communities and their importance in the lives of young people.[12] Interestingly, these "authoritative communities" sound encouragingly similar to the best expression of the church.[13] Of course, this is not even considering the best part—when we calculate the mystical, grace-giving nature of the church, along with the transformative work of the Spirit that centers on these people, we *must* seek to connect young people to this body and not simply to a ministry that is a subset of this body!

So much that has been passed off as youth ministry has not seemed to focus on integrating young people into the body of Christ. Think of the purpose or mission statement of a youth ministry. What does it say? Does it even have any communal elements? Does it focus on connecting youth to the historic and catholic body of Christ? In a quick web search, I found these statements:

- We exist to help young people start, develop, and grow into a personal relationship with Jesus Christ.[14]
- We exist to win, build, and equip young people in Christ.[15]
- We recognize the importance of inspiring the next generations for Jesus Christ. Passing this faith to children and youth is both a great responsibility and an incredible privilege. We are advo-

cates for our youth, helping them to be critical thinkers and to reach their own generation and the world around them.[16]

Instead, many seek to get youth to do or not do particular behaviors. For example, to pray a particular prayer or get them "saved" or to get them to regularly attend a worship service or youth meeting or to get them to come to camp. Not surprisingly, the unspecified goals are also to avoid premarital sex, drugs, and alcohol.

Doing or not doing these things is good and healthy, *but* it is not enough for an entire profession—youth ministry—to commit itself to, and I believe it's less than what God calls women and men to do with their lives.

Instead, and especially as we consider the dropout rate of active youth group attenders after graduating from high school,[17] I want to suggest that our aim (think *telos*) is to connect youth to the body of Christ. How is this done? Through helping youth build intentional relationships with nonfamilial adults with whom they can share life. Andy Root calls these authentic relationships of equality "place-sharing."[18] What makes a relationship of "place-sharing" is that it is a genuine relationship without an agenda. It is one of give and take, in which each person is vulnerable, invested, and authentically themselves.

Root contrasted this with a relationship of influence where the adult comes to the relationship with an agenda, typically of "salvation" or to convince the young person of their need to attend youth group, church, or a camp.

Smith and Lundquist, in their 2005 study, insisted that this relationship with a non-parental adult is "consistently part of the combination of factors during adolescence that correlate" with that continued connection to the church.[19] Root reframed the job of youth minister and suggested that their job is to "provide all adolescents with meaningful relationships of place-sharing with adults in the congregation."[20]

In this way, the youth minister is not an activity leader, *per se,* but one who facilitates intentional intergenerational relationships. The

activities are simply a means to connect youth to adults in the congregation, and not an end. In fact, if caring, committed, Christian adults are
not present, invested, and involved in the gatherings of the youth group,
then perhaps what is taking place is *not* ministry.

The point of these relationships is in the relationships themselves.
One possible test of that aim is to ask what happens to the relationship
if the young person drops out of involvement? Does the adult continue
to be connected (and provide connection by virtue of their relationship)
to the body of Christ? Does the adult continue to seek the young person
simply because they care—without an agenda to necessarily "come to
church"?

These are difficult, and yet important, distinctions that Root challenges us to consider, because they make a world of difference between
genuinely caring for other humans or attempting to get them to do something for you.

Fuller Youth Institute calls these place-sharing relationships
"sticky."[21] This is an intentional adjective because these relationships
are a significant factor to a young person remaining connected to the
body of Christ after youth group.

Think about it. Who is better able to keep in touch with and pray
for a recent youth group graduate—the busy, often-overworked youth
minister (or even the youth group volunteers), or other adults in the congregation in a place-sharing relationship with the young person?

To integrate young people into the body of Christ means spending two to four years or more with them, getting them meaningfully
connected in intentional intergenerational relationships that last beyond
their middle and high school years. It's about helping them to find their
"place" in the congregation. Perhaps it's about finding a ministry job to
keep them involved, but most of all it is about relationships with caring,
committed, Christian adults who will make space for them in their lives.

#4—"And the Mission of Christ"

"Missions" is a popular topic in much of youth ministry and the church. Many churches "send" people on trips to do good work, share life, and preach the gospel. I have certainly found trips transformative. These can be good for both those going and those receiving. However, what I refer to in this section is less about sending on a trip and more about "being sent" as a way of life.[22] How do we do this? How do we model it through our lives and every aspect of our ministry?

God is a missionary God. We think about this in terms of the *missio Dei* or the "mission of God." God is a missionary God because God is "a centrifugal Being."[23]

"Centrifugal" means "moving away from center."[24] Rather than staying centered with the Father and Spirit, Jesus the Son comes to us. This action of the *kenotic* (self-emptying) nature is best illustrated through the life, death, and resurrection of Jesus, who came to seek and save the least and lost. The hymn in Philippians 2:5–11 captures this truth beautifully. Paul wrote about Jesus:

Who, being in very nature God, did not consider equality with God something to be used to his own advantage; rather, he made himself nothing by taking the very nature of a servant, being made in human likeness. And being found in appearance as a man, he humbled himself by becoming obedient to death—even death on a cross! Therefore God exalted him to the highest place and gave him the name that is above every name, that at the name of Jesus every knee should bow, in heaven and on earth and under the earth, and every tongue acknowledge that Jesus Christ is Lord, to the glory of God the Father.

Christ came to us and, in so doing, set the example for how his followers are to live as an expression of that same missionary love. Rather than staying centered in the Trinitarian relationship in heaven, Jesus moved away from center and outward to his creation and thus to us. This is the mission of God.*

One of Jesus's clearest pronouncements of the focus of that missionary love is found in Luke's Gospel, the fourth chapter. Just before this passage, Jesus was tempted in the desert for forty days by the devil. I have always found the NIV's understatement of that event humorous: "He ate nothing during those days, and at the end of them he was *hungry*" (v. 2).

You think so? After that incredible encounter, Jesus headed back to his hometown and began his public ministry. Luke wrote:

He went to Nazareth, where he had been brought up, and on the Sabbath day he went into the synagogue, as was his custom. He stood up to read, and the scroll of the prophet Isaiah was handed to him. Unrolling it, he found the place where it is written:

"The Spirit of the Lord is on me, because he has anointed me to proclaim good news to the poor. He has sent me to proclaim freedom for the prisoners and recovery of sight for the blind, to set the oppressed free, to proclaim the year of the Lord's favor."

Then he rolled up the scroll, gave it back to the attendant and sat down. The eyes of everyone in the synagogue were fastened on him. He began by saying to them, "Today this scripture is fulfilled in your hearing." (4:10-21)

Christ's words convey a clear direction, a clear sense of vocation for his life. Similarly, those who follow this Jesus should not just be focused on a better place in the hereafter, but participate in the mission he began through the Father. This "mission" is for us. A relationship with Christ Jesus is not for later, it is for now—and it is about our whole selves doing everything motivated by that same love and purpose of Jesus. His mission involved a life of being sent.

---

*Alternatively, missional literature and theology also talk about the centripetal nature of God's love, drawing us back to the body. Perhaps the mission of God is about more than just going out but is ultimately about bringing all of creation into right relationship.

As N. T. Wright claims, we are to be both "instruments" as well as "agents" of God's new creation—this mission—of "putting the world to rights."[25] Any focus less than this is to short-change what Jesus has done for us and for the world. Yes, Jesus came to "save" us (the whole of creation), but this salvation is so much more than eternal life spent in heaven after death. Rather, it is about life eternal that begins now. It is about real and abundant life like we have never known—truly the good life! It is about being agents of God's redeeming work on earth now! This is what should get us up in the morning and be on our minds when we go to bed at night—participating with God in what God is doing on earth now, through the Spirit.

How much of this kind of visioning is done for our young people and their families in our ministries? Often, I fear our "vision" for the lives of our young people is much too small.

In the book *Perspectives on Family Ministry*, Jay Strother described the process in his ministry of shifting to a "family-equipping" model of youth and family ministry.[26] He discovered through surveying parents of his youth group that their vision for their children's lives was to be "happy."[27] So, these affluent parents in one of America's richest neighborhoods pushed their children into stress-filled lives, characterized by many extracurricular activities, high-pressured, advanced academic courses, and specialized athletics. Why? To get into good colleges, of course, in order to get good jobs, all to make good money—to what end? So they can be happy.[28]

These responses were the same from nominally Christian parents and those who were committed Christians. The *mission* these parents had for their children's entire lives seems at odds with the vision of Jesus. This does not make them bad parents; it just reveals the need to expand the church's understanding of vocation. The irony that Strother reveals is that the young people themselves, while acknowledging their affluence and comfort, openly reject the pressures, stress, and strain they see their parents face to obtain and maintain this affluence and comfort.

In the disturbing and accurate evaluation of the American church fueled by the research of the National Study of Youth and Religion, Kenda Dean wrote:

After two and a half centuries of shacking up with "the American dream," churches have perfected a dicey codependence between consumer-driven therapeutic individualism and religious pragmatism. These theological proxies gnaw, termite-like, at our identity as the body of Christ, eroding our ability to recognize that Jesus's life of self-giving love directly challenges the American gospel of self-fulfillment and self-actualization. Young people in contemporary culture prosper by following the latter. Yet Christian identity, and the "crown of rejoicing" that Wesley believed accompanied consequential faith born out of a desire to love God and neighbor, requires the former.[29]

Youth ministry that enlarges both the vision of young people and families for their lives is one that lasts—and that matters. If families are the center of a young person's life, which, for many, is reality until they are old enough to move outside of that center, then perhaps in some ways, moving away from center is a part of what it means to follow Christ. This does not mean to forsake family, by any means, but rather develop an individuation or differentiation from family that includes a vision for life that may be larger and more kenotic than the vision provided by the family of origin. Part of what comprises healthy and sustainable (youth) ministry is to develop a sense of vocation.

Vocation is used here to simply describe a person's lifework. In some corners of the well-intentioned church, there seems to have been a false hierarchy of value attributed to occupations. We seem to communicate that if a given person is an earnest Christian who wants to truly make a difference in the world, then they should become a missionary, or if that is not suitable, perhaps a pastor.[30] Of course, if either of those pursuits do not quite fit, then becoming a doctor or teacher may suffice since they will "help" others. But heaven forbid if a person should become a successful lawyer or businessperson—unless that person is a good tither!

Recapturing a proper view of vocation and making it a central pillar of youth ministry helps to reshape these well-intentioned but false understandings. John Stott wrote:

Jesus Christ calls all his disciples to "ministry," that is to service. He himself is the Servant par excellence, and he calls us to be servants too. This much then is certain: if we are Christians *we must spend our lives in the service of God and [humanity]*. The only difference between us lies in the *nature* of the service we are called to render. Some are indeed called to be missionaries, evangelists, or pastors, and others to the great professions of law, education, medicine, or the social sciences. Still others are called to commerce, to industry and farming, to accountancy and banking, to local government or parliament, to the mass media, or to homemaking and family building. In *all* these spheres, and many others besides, it is possible for Christians to interpret their lifework Christianly, and to see it neither as a necessary evil (necessary, that is, for survival), or even as a useful place in which to evangelize or make money for evangelism, but as their Christian vocation, as *the way Christ has called them to spend their lives in his service*. Further, a part of their calling will be to seek to maintain Christ's standards of justice, righteousness, honesty, human dignity and compassion in a society that no longer accepts them.[31]

Isn't that a refreshing vision of vocation? We can help young people assimilate that into their understanding of "what they want to be when they grow up" and help them consider that whatever they do in life can be done with a distinct bent toward loving God and loving others. The goal is not so much determining of what I "should" do, but considering the question of "what has God created me to do?" and then seeking to discover and experiment with what that might be. That will likely involve stops, starts, lurches—anything but a boring journey.

As Jeffrey Arnett asserts, the years from the late teens through the twenties is a time when "emerging adults can explore possibilities in love, work and world views."[32] But when found—and I don't believe there is necessarily only "one" thing—it will provide the most delicious fit and be filled with meaning, purpose, and direction for a person's life that will invite them to do their work with all of their heart, soul, mind, and strength. And in doing so, that person will live in the delightful rhythm of a daily kenotic beat of pouring out self for God and humanity—and the entire created order, as we work as God's redemptive agents putting the world to rights.

You may recognize that my view of the purpose of youth ministry is quite high and involves intentionally weaving young people into the historic community of faith. (In fact, one might argue the *telos* for which I'm arguing fits all of the efforts of the church called "ministry.") This view may be significantly different from the youth ministry with which you are familiar. That is not to say this is the "right" way and anything else is "wrong." I believe it is more a question of good, better, and best— meaning, what is the very "best" understanding of the purpose of youth ministry?

It all comes down to this for me: If I only have the attention of a typical young person for about forty hours in a given year,[33] then I want to make the very most of those forty hours. I am not interested in simply entertaining or keeping youth out of trouble; instead, I want to introduce them to a new way of living that offers eternal relationships with God's people and the most compelling vision and meaning for their existence as humans, a mission for their life. This is youth ministry that exists to integrate young people into the body of Christ and the mission of Christ.

TWO
Falling Forward
Transitioning to a Ministry That Integrates Young People into the Body of Christ and into the Mission of Christ
by Johnny Hampton[1]

● ● ● ● ● ● ● ● ● ● ● ● ●

As a way to offer some handles to these ideas, I've asked Johnny Hampton to share about his church's journey toward integration. —Michael A. Kipp

IN 2004 I BECAME the youth pastor at a church I had served as a volunteer, intern, and full-time ministry resident for six years—all with the youth ministry. Being a rookie youth pastor and having the weight of a large and successful ministry, coupled with high expectations, I was attentive to all details of the youth ministry . . . except one.

We always say, "Relationships are the backbone of our youth ministry." This is true. Relationships are key. We went to great lengths to build trust and interaction with many young people over the years, hoping for a chance to share Christ in some way. However, mainly I was trailblazing relational opportunities that were a dead-end trail to myself.

I was the youth pastor who wanted everyone to show up at youth group because *I* would be there, because they liked *me* and *my* youth ministry—which was the greatest thing since *my* invention of the Internet. The "relationship" I spent so much time trailblazing was one-dimensional. It ended at me, my youth ministry, my retreat, my mission trip, and even in the bleachers of many extracurricular activities.

The most significant "relationship" needed was one between the young person and the body and mission of Christ. This is the one detail I should have paid attention to, but as the philosophy of my ministry was played out through the nine years of seventh graders I saw go through our youth group, the lack of integration into the body and mission of Christ became an increasing point of conviction for me. This conviction was exposed in several ways.

Besides the national studies highlighting the numbingly low percentage of high school graduates who remain a part of the church during their young adult years, we began to recognize defects in our ministry leadership. I do not mean our leaders were incapable of effective ministry; our leadership was so focused on ministry "silos" that we were not able to see the big picture.

Imagine a field with many silos, each holding an ingredient that is key to making the most perfect snickerdoodle cookie ever tasted. In one is butter, in another, sugar, then eggs, flour, baking soda, salt, more sugar, cinnamon, and then one with the secret ingredient that pushes it from an average snickerdoodle to an *epic* snickerdoodle. Now the only problem is that these silos are closed off from each other.

Individually, these ingredients are fine, nothing is wrong with them. They are good, and each silo holds an integral part of the cookie. But alone, without the possibility of being thrown into the same bowl and mixed up to create the perfect complement to one another . . . well, then we will never have a snickerdoodle. It is just a bunch of quality ingredients. The components have to work together to create the perfect cookie.

Another defect was in the motivation behind my leadership. A lot of our efforts were one-dimensional—get as many students to participate in our ministries and events as possible, and get them there often. We were performance-driven rather than mission-driven.

I will never forget when my character as a leader was exposed. We were preparing for an annual retreat that we put a lot of time, energy, and resources into. This retreat had been my baby for years. We were promoting it, pushing students to attend, and telling them it would be "the best one yet!"

I was pleading with one individual to attend the retreat. He had signed up, but then had to back out. The reason? His family decided to attend his grandparents' sixtieth wedding anniversary celebration in another state.

I fed him some lines about commitment, being a leader, setting an example, and gave other guilt-ridden reasons as to why he should attend the retreat instead. (Let us say a little prayer together: "Father, please forgive me for the times I became selfishly upset when a young person skipped out on youth group to volunteer in kids' church or in the nursery. Amen.")

I am so glad he decided to go celebrate with his family. It was absurd that I would try to talk any young person out of something like that. I had become so one-dimensionally hardwired that I was asking him to put his family aside to attend a retreat. Why? Because I wanted more people there. That is probably when I began wrestling with some difficult questions about the purpose and direction of *my* ministry.

A couple of years later, a gust of "wind" pushed me over the edge toward seriously aligning our ministries to integrate our families with the body and mission of Christ.

There was a time in my ministry when I cared more about the *give-away* a person would receive than the *person* who would receive the give-away. For instance, I recently saw a ten-year-old URSM (Upper Room Student Ministries, the name of our youth group) sweater worn by someone I have not talked to in about a decade. My first reaction was, unfortunately, "Cool, still representing the sweet sweater!"

While catching up with this former youth ministry participant, my mind reeled with the realization that this was another example of one who "got away." This was another person who had walked through our youth ministry—attended events, mission trips, and worship services—

and left wondering what to do with the church after high school graduation. I am so glad God works beyond my ignorance!

I learned that this young adult spent a few years wondering and wandering and has recently jumped back into an active leadership role in the church. "I see the retreat sweater is still holding up nicely for you," I joked.

He responded, "I have hung on to it all these years because, (a) it is comfortable, and (b) I have great memories from those years. It reminds me that there were people back then who loved and cared for me."

On one hand, that is cool—at least the sweater was a good reminder that he was loved. But how much more significant would this person's journey have been if he had a *person—or better yet, several people*—to remind him of how loved he is, instead of a pre-shrunk-cotton souvenir? The best giveaway is our time and investment into intentional intergenerational relationships—a giveaway that will never be outgrown.

Shortly after that conversation, a chain of events eventually led us to where we are now, offering a healthier, more unified, and missionally focused ministry. Only three years after transitioning to a ministry that integrates children, young people, and families into the body and mission of Christ, we are slowly breaking old habits, forming new ones, and learning daily how to take Deuteronomy 6:4–9 seriously in our church and homes.

Transition has not always been easy. Some moments it has felt like trying to build a house out of water. It took *a lot* of work. With that said, this transition has been smooth. By the grace of God, we took the right steps to help our church make this transition in a way that developed desire, ownership, and motivation to see our mission accomplished.

We took many steps along the way, some of which were very contextual. There were intuitive steps I took because I understood the heartbeat of our church, yet those steps might not fit in another context. So what follows are the "essential" steps we took to making this a successful transition in our ministry.

Metamorphosis and Implementation

Preparing the Soil

One of the most consistent blunders a leader makes is rushing the process. The soil had been tilled for years before we were ready to make this change. Much of this tilling was happening without our knowing it, and the timing was right. I did not go to sleep on Sunday night, and wake up on Monday morning with a new idea to try that week. This had been brewing for years.

We had begun trying to recover our struggling young adult ministry, hoping to salvage anyone we could as people started slipping from our grip. We wondered if we did not have enough going on for young adults after they graduated from high school. So we added a ministry (small-group social activities and a part-time paid pastor) for them. That helped, but it was more of a bandage than a sustainable solution. We continued to search for answers, but when we became honest about the solution, we knew this was a change deeper than just sending a mass email.

Preparing the soil involved many important elements, but *perhaps the most essential element was the journey I took with my lead pastor* through this process. I knew if he was not with me, this transition would only go so far. Fortunately, he was supportive and trusting.

I am so thankful for a lead pastor who listened and processed my ideas. He would tell me when to leave and close the door on the way out, and at other times, he dropped important work he was doing to ask me to close the door, come in, and sit down. He was willing to grasp this vision and have my back. Having a solid, supporting cast is essential to making this a healthy transition.

Another element to preparing the soil, and something that was essential to helping this be a smooth transition, was my *ministry longevity in one location*. I realize some steps I took were only possible because our congregation had a level of trust and respect that I'd earned throughout a decade and a half of ministry with one church. However, having a lot of trust and respect can also be a dangerous place to live.

Because I had been with this church for so long, and because I was so gung-ho about this change, a lot of people were on board fairly quickly. So much of the "soil preparation" involved prayer and discernment. I had to be certain this was a "God thing" and not a "Johnny thing."

Timing Is Everything

The soil was prepared. Then, the opportunity presented itself. After our children's pastor resigned, our lead pastor, children's leadership team (CLT), and church board quickly made plans to search for our next children's pastor. Before the first meeting between our lead pastor and the CLT, I approached our lead pastor with some questions (remember, he was used to my crazy ideas). We had been talking about this new-to-us way of leading our age-level ministries, but had not really known how to implement those ideas. So, I asked if we could start by asking the CLT some questions—just planting some seeds to see where they would take us. He agreed and invited me to that first meeting to share my heart and vision.

I walked into the room at that first meeting, and the first words a member of the CLT said were, "What are you doing at this meeting? You are the youth pastor!"

"Exactly," I responded.

After they spent forty-five minutes deliberating what steps to take to begin a search for the next children's pastor, our lead pastor turned the floor over to me. The next ten minutes were the first ten minutes of what we now call family ministry at our church. I began asking questions that provoked us to *lead our ministry out of imagination rather than out of memory.*

Part of the soil preparation was realizing if we wanted to integrate young people into the body and mission of Christ, then waiting to start until a young person was in seventh grade was too late. This is a lifelong, family-mentor, church-body effort that exists from the cradle to the grave.

I walked out of that meeting as the "interim staff advisor to the children's ministry"—translation: "You can be the children's pastor *and* the youth pastor at the same time, right?" Remember what I said about this transition being *a lot* of work?

That night, the CLT committed to meet with me several times to discern the direction we should go. Those follow-up meetings developed an even deeper sense of affirmation, much of it through good—and not so good—questions being asked. Nonetheless, all the questions helped expose why we needed to have this conversation.

Questions, Meetings, and Consensus

Another essential part of this transition was letting people ask questions. *Questions should not scare us.* If people are not asking questions, they probably do not care, or you are not doing anything worth asking about. If they are asking questions, take advantage of the opportunity to have a conversation.

We were asked a lot of questions along the way, and while I thought I knew what the questions would be ahead of time, and even had some answers nailed down, it was a discipline for me to unpack some of the answers with the people who asked questions and help instill ownership. I was often surprised at the depth of the answers that we discovered together versus some of the shallow answers I had formed on my own.

Some questions asked were:

- "Who will be my child's pastor?"
- "Is there research to back this up?"
- "Will you make us do everything together?"
- "Will there still be children's and youth ministry separately?"
- "Will my kid have to go to church (worship service) with me now?"
- "How do we keep our pastors, staff, and volunteers from burning out?"
- "What will this cost (literally and figuratively)?"

These questions led to a lot of meetings. When I first started researching intergenerational ministry, I stumbled onto the ReThink Group and the Think Orange movement. I clicked on their website and saw that Reggie Joiner was the leader. The materials looked exactly like what I was thinking about, so I emailed him to see if I could pick his brain. Did I mention earlier how utterly myopic my vision of youth ministry was in our local church? I was so nearsighted that I sincerely thought I would pave the way for something new and unseen.

Reggie put me in touch with several other pastors who had made this transition, and each told me, "Prepare for a *ton* of meetings. If you cannot handle sitting in a lot of meetings, sharing your vision, answering the same questions, asking the same questions, hearing the same doubts, being challenged the same way, over and over again, it will be a long, painful road. So, just be prepared and embrace it. You will be in more meetings over the next six months than you have over the past six years."

No truer words had ever been spoken to me. However, I quickly learned that the time I took for these meetings was *essential* to the success of this transition. I met with parents, board members, staff members, volunteers, youth group members, children, families, janitors, community leaders, more parents, more board members, more staff . . . well, you get the point. What was the point of all of those meetings? Consensus. Questions led to meetings, and meetings led to consensus.

Consensus is essential to a successful transition. Consensus did not mean that everyone agreed, but it meant that everyone was willing to give it a shot. They were willing to trust our leadership, make an effort with us to do the best we could do, and would support us, rather than sit back and watch to see if we would fail.

Through the questions, meetings, and gaining consensus, we learned how we should communicate this vision to the church and take the next strategic steps forward. In fact, the meetings became the *de facto* way the vision was communicated—sort of a slow spread rather than a dramatic announcement. That method ended up being much more effective.

Preach It

When we were prepared to take our vision from beta testing and meeting with shareholders, it was time to start sharing with the church as a whole. Just for a point of reference, that first meeting I had with the CLT was in October 2010. I spent four weeks meeting with people—digging trenches, building mounds, planting seeds . . . more soil preparation. The first time I preached about this vision was in November 2010, the Sunday before the first board meeting where the CLT would present a proposal to the church board.

The purpose of this sermon was simply to engage the body in the vision and get them to entertain the idea that there are possibilities outside of the box. At that point the goal was simply to get them to recognize that there was perhaps something better than what we were doing. Working with several of the pastors, I crafted a sermon focusing on the influence our church, families, community, mentors, and friends can have on our children, youth, and each other. Mark 3:31–34 helps us to begin thinking about who our family really is and who else can be family:

> Then Jesus' mother and brothers arrived. Standing outside, they sent someone in to call him. A crowd was sitting around him, and they told him, "Your mother and brothers are outside looking for you."
>
> "Who are my mother and my brothers?" he asked.
>
> Then he looked at those seated in a circle around him and said, "Here are my mother and my brothers! Whoever does God's will is my brother and sister and mother."

We simply started the process of reshaping perspective on what the church should look like. After that sermon, it was back to the grind—more meetings, questions, wrestling.

More Meetings and Asking the Right Questions

Our next essential step was for the CLT to present to the church board this vision and what was now *their* desire to see this transition. The goal of this meeting was not for final approval. We still had much hard work to do in communicating this transition to our church and engaging them in the process.

On the Tuesday night following that sermon, our board listened to the heart of our CLT, and then I was able to share my heart as well. We spent much time exposing the problem. We shared all of the ugly stats about young people leaving the church after high school, shallow discipleship, lack of ability to articulate the faith, family engagement, etc. We easily made the case that we needed to do something different. We were not satisfied with how many of our teens had disappeared after high school, and our questions focused on why we thought the youth were *leaving* the church: "Why do you think students are leaving?" "Are we not relevant to them?" "Is the worship not good enough?" "Should the pastor wear skinny jeans, and preach with a coffee mug in hand?"

This is where I helped our church begin to take a critical turn in the tone of our conversation. I inverted those questions with a simple, yet revealing question. Instead of asking why youth were *leaving* the church, I asked, "Why are some *staying* with the church?"

If we try to figure out why people do not stay with the church, we will be all over the map. However, by looking at the success stories, we begin to understand what *is* working. Once we have those answers, then we will be able to answer the question, "What does intergenerational ministry look like?" or "What does it look like to integrate young people into the body and mission of Christ?"

Doing this will give us stories to tell that will instantly connect people to our vision and the outcomes we are aiming for. There is power in story, and when people can connect to a story, they will connect with the vision.

When we began asking the question, "Why are they still here?" our church discovered three main reasons. One, they had incredibly strong family ties within the church. Their whole family was engaged in significant ways throughout the church. Two, they had at least one (often several) caring, committed Christian adults who had invested in them *outside* of the programs of the youth ministry. Many of the young adults who were still around after high school did not have any other family members attending our church, but they had mentors who were their spiritual family.

The third reason we discovered high school graduates were still around was because they were consistently connected and committed to serving in a ministry within the church. They had a community connection *outside* of the youth ministry.

These initial identifiers gave us a solid foundation to build on as we began aiming at our ultimate goal.

Ridiculously Redundant

When we had board approval (and buy-in) to our vision, we continued to meet with key people, get feedback, and hone in on how we would communicate this to the church as a whole. We sent a letter to every person in our database explaining in short, almost like a verbal trailer, our vision and desire to meet with everyone to share more details and provide an opportunity for feedback and discussion.

We held *the same* meeting four times over four weeks. My goal was to make sure everyone had an opportunity to learn more and share their concerns. By this time, because we had invested so much time talking with people before these meetings, there was a good chance that people who had already begun engaging in this process would be at each meeting. This was essential because when the difficult questions were asked, I was not the only one answering questions. Others would share their opinions.

Was it redundant to have the same meeting four times? Probably. Was it worth it? Absolutely. That process gave people a voice. Even if we had the best idea in the world, if we had not given people a chance to talk about it, ask their questions, and give their feedback, it would not have been as well received as it was. As I said earlier, consensus is critical, and these meetings were *the* most essential element to our building consensus moving into this transition. Again, this did not mean everyone agreed with everything we proposed, but it is hard to turn a giant ship, especially when people are not on the ship to begin with. At the very least, we got them on the ship throughout the course of these four meetings. Now it was time to begin organizing ourselves to accomplish our mission.

Strategy with an End in Mind

Organizing to the Win

After the "final four" meetings, and after the "big dance" with the church board to seek and receive final approval for our family ministry, it was time to take seriously a common-sense, but often overlooked, principle in leadership: to "organize to the win."[2]

So what is our win? Our big picture win is to integrate children, young people, families, and everyone who is a part of our fellowship into the body and mission of Christ. As our family ministry began taking shape, our target was one of the early essentials that we had to keep in mind. What is our target? In ministry, we can get bogged down with the details of this year, month, week, and (deep breath) sometimes it is all we can do just to get through today, right?

I knew it would be difficult, but if we wanted to do something that would make an impact beyond today, tomorrow, next week, next month, or next year, then we needed to start thinking about a strategy that considered even the baby who had just been born in our church family.

For the baby in our church who was just introduced for the first time—how will that child be integrated into the body and mission of Christ? That kind of question rattles our cages a little because we are so wired to think only about the five, six, or seven years they are in our specific age area ministries. But how would our age-level ministries change if we had the entire scope of discipleship of a child's life in mind?

I have two boys. If all goes as planned, one will graduate in 2025 and the other will graduate in 2029. So, the question for us is not what is on the calendar next month, but what role do we want the class of

2025, 2029, 2035, and beyond to have in the church when they graduate from high school?

If we are honest, realigning our vision, our structure, and our ministries to that win is a difficult task, because it takes more than re-structuring of an organization chart to make it happen. Changing a title to intergenerational, generations, connections, intergen-min, orange, or family ministry pastor will not automatically get everything to align as it should. It will require a cultural change (more like a revolution!) within your church; it causes the DNA of who you are as a church to mutate. That can be a grueling process, but it is worth it and needs to happen.

So, we began organizing to the win. We spent the next six months, April to September, forming our leadership teams, realigning our ministry areas with a common end in mind, and then officially launching our family ministry that fall, nearly one year after walking into that CLT meeting for the first time.

In hindsight, one year is not a long time to process a transition like this, and while we may have launched into this new way of doing ministry in only one year, that will probably be too fast for some churches. As I mentioned earlier, longevity played a huge role in this process—we were able to push things along rather quickly because of the significant trust and relationship I had built with our church over the years. I should also mention that by the one-year mark, we were still far from where we needed to be organizationally, but we at least had traction and momentum to keep the ball rolling.

Leadership Structure

I am blessed to be leading a family ministry team consisting of an early childhood director, learning center (day care) director, children's pastor, youth pastor, family ministry interns, and a small army of core paid staff and volunteer leaders. While the structure of our leadership and scope of our ministry will evolve over time, this is the initial structure that is working to help us organize to the win.

Putting this team together was no small task. Each of those positions existed in some way before we began this transition; however, those leaders rarely met in the same room at the same time. We are just a few years into this process now, and I think it is safe to say that up to this point, perhaps the most "essential" essential is that we have made it a point to have a consistent weekly team meeting. When we first started doing this, it was awkward. If something was being discussed that only had to do with one area of ministry, the others in the room would start side conversations about their own areas. It took time for us to understand that whatever the children's ministry was discussing was impacting what was happening in the youth ministry—and vice versa. It started to develop a team mentality. We began establishing a value that each area of ministry was a vital part of what comes before and after in the discipleship path for our ministry. We began speaking a common language and planning our ministries together.

One significant and practical outcome of our team meetings was that we decided to create and plan one yearly calendar together. When we started planning our calendar, we discovered how redundant many of our ministries were and in how many directions we were pulling families, often on the same night during the same hours. For instance, when we looked at doing a fall harvest party, in light of our newfound vision of intergenerational ministry, we thought it was a bit ridiculous that the previous year we had done three different harvest parties as a church over the span of three consecutive days.

Beginning to See Fruit

Outcomes

While we still have much to learn and many ways to continue this transition, we are starting to see some fruit and are encouraged by the ways our people are "getting it." We are seeing more families take the initiative in discipling their children. There is a growing sense of desire to interact with other generations. We are beginning to tell stories about intergenerational ministry that we had always wished we could tell—stories of generational walls being broken down and ministry lines being blurred.

Recently, an eighty-one-year-old decided he wanted to volunteer with our middle school ministry. His interest in helping our seventh- and eighth-grade students was sparked because of a commitment he made to pray for one of our young adult interns. His prayers led to his wanting to invest more in her life and ministry. That led to his wanting to join her ministry efforts. The next thing we knew, an eighty-one-year-old man had a crowd of middle school students around him, hanging on his every word. Senior adult, young adult, early adolescent—now that is a beautiful circle of relationship.

Recently, our congregation was blessed to hear a saint in our church pray for a young man who had just graduated from high school. This was not the first time this elderly man had prayed for this young man. He had committed to pray for this young man when he was in first grade. It was a rich, sincere prayer filled with compassion—the kind of prayer that was the culmination of years and years of praying for this young man as if he were sending his own child out for the very first time. Just a couple of weeks ago, my first grader received a handwritten letter from his new prayer partners—a couple that has attended our church for forty-four years. This story will tell itself over and over for years to come.

On a Wednesday night, our five-year-olds were learning a lesson on what it means to serve. The teacher had just finished the lesson when one of the children looked out the window and saw some youth ministry members walking around with a trash bag. He promptly asked the teacher about it.

The teacher could have easily explained what was happening and let the kids get back to throwing toys. Instead, she capitalized on a significant opportunity. She gathered the class, lined them up, and walked them outside. The teacher asked the group to explain what they were doing. They talked about the compassionate service they were doing, why they were walking around the neighborhood picking up trash, and they spent some time with the kids helping out.

Once more, the lines were blurred. A child *listened* to the teacher talk about serving. A child *learned* from people who were doing what the teacher was explaining. A child *lived* out what he heard and learned—all because a teacher was willing to blur the lines . . . willing to seize the opportunity.

For eight weeks our senior high class partnered with an adult Sunday school class and spent time building relationships, digging into the Bible, praying together, encouraging one another, and becoming present in each other's lives in the context of the Sunday school setting. It was not just the adults investing in the students; it was a mutual encounter. In fact, on one Sunday during a worship service, one of the adults from the Sunday school class went forward to pray about an issue in her life, and a young person who had been in her group that morning prayed with her. Since then, that mentoring relationship has blossomed. Once more, we blurred the lines and exposed what could happen when we integrate ourselves more fully into the body and mission of Christ.

These kinds of stories are being heard throughout our church more and more. As each new story is told, we are inspired by the way we see God's story playing out. When we enter God's story, the possibilities are limitless. When the stories dead-end at our programs, we have a hard time coming up with possibilities. With that in mind, our efforts are not to get people integrated into our family ministry. Rather, our family ministry is focused on giving children, youth, families, and adults the best chance they have to be integrated into the story of God, into the body and mission of Christ.

This has not been an easy road, and we have much work to do as we continue to nurture more ways of practicing effective, intergenerational ministry. However, I am more hopeful than ever before that we are headed in the right direction.

SECTION II
INTEGRATION STARTS WITH YOU!
TOWARD HEALTH, LONGEVITY, AND STRUCTURE

The cycle of dysfunctional relationships between senior pastors and youth pastors must be broken. Youth pastors must learn how to commit themselves to uniquely prioritizing this relationship.
—Ron King[1]

Doug Fields, arguably the most widely respected youth worker in the country, told his senior pastor that it would take *five years* (five years!) before the church could expect to see fruit from the youth ministry he'd be leading.
—*Sustainable Youth Ministry*[2]

The mean length of tenure in a youth ministry position of all participants was 4.7 years.
—Jonathan Grenz[3]

Nothing so conclusively proves a [person's] ability to lead others as what [they do] from day to day to lead [themselves].
—Thomas Watson[4]

THREE
Exegeting the Community
The Importance of Integration
with Pastor and Community
• • • • • • • • • • • •

I'LL NEVER FORGET the day my favorite seminary professor told us a deep truth: "You don't go to a good church, you go to a good lead pastor."

The importance of "fit" for a youth minister and church is a critical piece if integration will truly occur in a church. The youth minister must have (or develop) a sense of their own integration into a community if ever the young people will.

In many contexts that means the lead pastor and the youth pastor must have some sort of chemistry. That is imperative then in my own denominational context: the Church of the Nazarene. Because of the church polity,[1] the pastoral staff works for the pastor.[2] Only the pastor works for the "church," by being responsible to the church board (substitute elder board, session, etc.). In other words, technically, the pastoral staff is not directly responsible to the church board but to the lead pastor. This makes a person's relationship with that leader vital to the job satisfaction, longevity, and potential effectiveness.

Further, if the senior leader chooses to resign (or is fired), all church pastoral staff must submit letters of resignation. Although potentially scary, this does not necessarily mean that all staff will need to find new jobs. I've been a staff person who has been "rehired" by new lead pastors without any interruption of my ministerial role. In fact, it's not uncommon for pastoral staff to be retained, at least through the transition, but it does create a unique situation once the new leader is hired.

Whatever you may think of this structure, it does two things: allows new leadership to truly begin "anew" and makes the relationships between the senior leader and associate pastors critical.

Although your context may be very different, a key relationship for the youth minister who seeks integration into the body of Christ must begin with an eye focused on their personal integration.

In the spring of the year I would graduate from seminary, I reflected on lessons learned from serving as a volunteer youth worker while in college and for two different three-year, full-time stints at two churches during the previous six-plus years.

During my time as a volunteer, I had run my own painting business with six employees, and I made great money as a twenty-two-year-old. So, I understood that I could make money through hard work. My seminary education taught me much about the Bible, church history, theology, philosophy, and, thankfully, about the practice of ministry as well. In fact, one professor in my pastoral theology course really helped me nail down some key parts of my own philosophy of ministry. I drafted what became known as my "Important Concessions for Lifelong Commitment to Youth Ministry," which I am sharing here:

Assumptions with which I come:

- This is the last church I intend to serve in ministry.
- Typically, only modest gains are made in an associate's compensation package (categories below), which is a major reason staff people leave churches.
- I desire to make a long-term investment in this church, community, region, state, and our world.
- Transformation in a ministry requires not a one- to two-year investment but rather a three- to five-year timeline.

As a result of these assumptions, and based upon my experience in business and seven years as a youth worker, I perceive the following as important concessions for the best chance at longevity.

Time Off

- At minimum, one day off per week.
- One personal day per month (nonaccumulating).
- Four weeks of paid vacation per year (week defined as seven days with one Sunday included).
- The opportunity to take a sabbatical after five years and each fifth year thereafter (minimum of six weeks).

Professional Development

- Opportunity to preach in the primary worship service once per quarter.
- Flexibility to speak at camps and retreats (increasing flexibility over time).
- Opportunities for continued education/conference attendance annually (church to pay in full, if budget allows).

Compensation

- Based upon experience, education, and commensurate with regional and/or national averages.
- Health insurance provided.
- Retirement plan provided (matching plan preferred).
- Expense account (or other budget) provided for hospitality, professional books, and other ministry-related costs.

Accountability

- I will provide my supervisor with a weekly plan for how I plan to spend my time so that they will know where I am and how I am investing my time.
- This plan will be evaluated and updated annually (if needed) and discussed in my annual review.

Finances

Although a bit bold (even brash) at times, the core of this treatise is solid. When I graduated from college in 1993 with a bachelor of science in business management, peers of mine went to work for large organizations, making nearly $50,000 a year. I went to work for a church and lived in an apartment connected to the church building and received less than $5,000 a year. That was okay, and God was incredibly faithful through that time and continues to provide for my family and me in unimaginable ways.

However, that experience, and many others in the intervening years, taught me that church leaders do not always pay their staff competitive wages. Their hearts are not bad, but in seeking to be good "stewards," they can actually be bad stewards of personnel as a staff person will leave within a few years due, in part, to inadequate compensation. Don't get me wrong, I have no illusion that I will get rich working for God's people; I just think I shouldn't have to be poor, either.

What I believed back in 1998 and have come to recognize, in reflection and through research, is the wisdom beyond my years those assumptions contained. If the vision of integration is to happen, the *longevity* of the youth worker is a key component. You may recall how Johnny had served at College Church nine years before making the shift toward integration. Eugene Peterson wrote a book, *A Long Obedience in a Single Direction*, and in it he describes the transformation that can come both personally and professionally through time and relationship. I think we all know this to be true and may have a story or two of ambitious pastor friends who went to a new church and tried to change too much too soon—and in no time were looking for a new church.

The salary paid to the youth minister is a common barrier to longevity (and thus the vision for integration). The problem comes in discerning, "What is a fair and reasonable salary?" This is a key to longevity because too often, enthusiastic youth workers hungry for their first job and thrifty church leaders agree on a salary that does not always represent livable income.

Sometime in the future, when this person marries or has a child (or second or third child), and the costs of living rise (which they do each year, by the way), this youth worker may have no other recourse to grow their income besides doing outside work, taking on more responsibility, or finding a different job. Money is the root cause of too many youth workers (and other church staff) leaving churches. Though it may not be easy, this challenge can be solved by youth workers educating themselves about a livable wage in their context.

Thankfully, numerous resources provide help for this important question. One is the *Group Magazine* annual youth minister's compensation survey and report. Every year Group Publishing surveys youth ministers from around the country and reports averages of salary by metrics such as: experience, education, size of church, part of the country, and more.

Another resource by Christianity Today, Inc., is its annual compensation report.[2] These helpful resources should be consulted. Also, I encourage youth ministers to research what their local public school district pays teachers who have the same amount of education and full-time experience. This information is usually available online and is categorized by education and experience (often indicated as "steps").

It can help to contextualize a salary in light of the various costs of living in different parts of the country (and even within some states). This can be a helpful guideline to measure if the salary offer of a church is "reasonable." Of course, public school teachers are off-contract for a few months each year, and so to look at what they are compensated and add ten percent or more is reasonable.

Teachers are not always compensated particularly well, but this kind of scale provides a helpful, contextual metric in considering a salary offer—and makes it clear that a potential staff person is not all about the money, but about seeking a sustainable wage.

The other part of this is asking about a church's practice of providing annual (or even occasional) cost of living adjustments (COLAs). Because of inflation, a salary today has less buying power (to purchase goods and services) each year due to rising prices. If churches don't slowly raise their employees' wages, over time those salaries essentially shrink.

Several years ago, our church established a salary schedule like those of our local schools. It was an attempt to ensure that pastoral staff members were paid at least a *minimum* livable wage. At the time it meant that a few of our staff received raises because their compensation was below the level we set for a pastor with their education and experience. Of course, pastors can negotiate a higher salary, which is great! But that's not typical for someone in the earlier years of ministry. The idea with the salary schedule was to create a minimum acceptable wage and to build in annual increases as the church budget allowed.

It also provided incentives, in terms of a higher step on the scale for further education and even being ordained—not that a higher salary is the proper motivation for either of these, but the point is to recognize the achievement and value it creates in a staff person.

Besides salary, there are other important considerations: vacation time, sick days, family medical leave (FMLA), comp time, retirement plan, etc. For a full-time position, health insurance (in some form) is a necessity, as is some expense account or budget from which to support the relational ministry and hospitality that are so important to connecting with others.

When I started in full-time ministry, the rule of thumb encouraged by financial planners was to set aside ten percent of your annual salary for retirement. I have preached and practiced a simple financial rule: tithe ten percent, then tithe ten percent to your retirement, and finally set aside five percent to savings and live off seventy-five percent of your salary.

This is not easy, but can be done. Today financial planners suggest setting aside fifteen percent of your annual salary for retirement. Whatever you do, get started now. Don't wait. There are many illustrations of the importance of beginning your retirement savings early in your career. Below is one example.[3]

If a person sets aside $250 per month in a retirement savings vehicle [such as a 401(k) or 403(b)], earns 8 percent annual interest on that money, and invests monthly until age 65, here is the amount of money that person will have if they start at the following ages:

25	-	$878,570
35	-	$375,073
40	-	$148,236

Crazy, right? This illustrates the time value of money due to compound interest, and it is astounding! Just one decade of additional time saving for retirement makes the difference between a comfortable retirement and working part-time during the "golden years." All this to say, get started saving, don't delay.

Regarding vacation leave, it is customary for associate pastors early in their careers to receive between two to three weeks of paid leave each year. I think this time off is a great place to negotiate, even in a person's early career, since it does not actually "cost" (in terms of real dollars) the church anything to provide additional vacation leave. It can be a useful tool when discussing compensation for a pastor to ask for an additional week of vacation, particularly after a favorable annual review and if an increased salary is not realistic.

Often churches may be cash poor, but they can offer an additional week (or two) of vacation to enhance a compensation package. Interestingly, European countries have a very different attitude about vacation time. It is not unusual for new workers to begin with as much as four or even six weeks of vacation and only a thirty-five-hour work week! The historic work ethic in the United States has encouraged hard work—often through longer work weeks and less vacation time. Interesting to note as well, workers with more vacation and shorter work weeks actually are more productive workers![4]

Expectations

Another key conversation before accepting any position is to seek clarity on what a given pastor expects in terms of the work week. In my experience, pastors range widely on this topic. I've heard or encountered attitudes from lead pastors that both they and their associates should work anywhere from forty to fifty-five hours each week. Some even more. Others simply require that the job gets done and are not as concerned about the number of hours a person is "at the church" or "working" each week. There are pros and cons on both sides. The point is to inquire and not be caught off guard by the expectations of the leader. Ask as part of the interview process,[5] and then decide if this place is right for you.

Professionalism

Once you're employed, present yourself in a professional manner in all situations. For too long, youth pastors have gone the lazy route and dressed sloppily, behaved poorly, and bolstered the stereotype of not being a "real" pastor by their lack of professionalism, both within and outside the church.

People respect professionalism. And your behavior represents both the church and the Savior, so it's critical to present yourself as a professional. That does not mean you can't have fun, but it may mean you need to wear long pants and closed-toed shoes—depending upon your context and the wishes of your lead pastor. Again, all of these things are best discovered in the interview process.

Other key parts of presenting yourself as a professional: communication (verbal and written), punctuality and preparation for meetings or appointments, general attire, and grooming (I know, I sound like your mom, now—but it's true!).

Communication

The way you communicate both verbally and in writing—even in texts or social media—matters. Do you take time to consider what you will say, how you will say it, and the tone of delivery? Or do you just verbally vomit your ideas on others? Do you consider your facial expression when others speak? Or does your face betray your immediate feelings?

Our consistent behavior builds impressions and images of us in others' minds, and there is no time like the present to shape those images in favorable ways. Written communication is easier because a plethora of tools is available to ensure its grammar and accuracy.

The bottom line is that you represent "your" ministry. You interact with others through your communication. Work to make it worthy of the young people and families with whom you minister. Communication also means to communicate often and accurately with your young people and families. Having or developing means for that exchange of information is another aspect of good communication.

Punctuality and Preparation

Another central part of professionalism is simply showing up when you are supposed to and being prepared. This is a simple way to demonstrate that you take your vocation seriously. Nothing is more frustrating to supervisors than staff members who are habitually late, unprepared, or sloppy in their work. Do all that you can to be prepared and good things, in time, will come.

Attire and Grooming

Early in my youth ministry career, at some level, I believed the falsehood that I wasn't a "real" pastor because I worked primarily with young people. One way that crept into my personae was in my attire and grooming. I didn't think much of my appearance and often didn't shave for days. My lead pastor gave me grace and never mentioned these things. He wore a suit and tie every day and although I do not think that is the pattern to follow, I do believe that wearing clean and neat clothes and properly grooming ourselves is the correct pattern. The way we look leaves an impression on others. When they find out we are a pastor (a real one), they form an impression about the church and our Savior. It's not necessary to dress elaborately each day, but we should dress in ways that do not distract others or draw undue attention to ourselves (whether good or bad).

Most days during the school year, I stand in front of a classroom of college students. Some dress very well; others have simply rolled out of bed and come to class. Those choices leave an impression on me about who they are and how seriously they take life at this point. Like it or not, how you dress and your personal appearance matters. So pay attention to this.

Health

Physical and Mental Health

My colleague at Northwest Nazarene University Dr. Joe Gorman wrote an excellent book on the importance of all aspects of our health entitled *Healthy, Happy, Holy: 7 Practices toward a Holistic Life*. In it, he wrote about his own journey of realizing how the demands of ministry and a growing family crowded out his responsibilities to care for his own body. All that came to a head when he was in his thirties and had a health scare that he believed was a heart attack.

Gorman noted that this was the genesis of a new way of living for him, and one that he discovered was more closely aligned with a true kingdom vision than how he was choosing to live before. Joe wrote:

My pseudo-heart attack set my life on a new trajectory. I tell my story about overcoming unhealthy habits to encourage you to take healthy steps in your own life before you possibly receive a similar wake-up call. My wake-up call helped me realize how vitally interconnected every area of my life is with the others. As a result, I no longer view my physical, mental, and emotional life as unrelated to my spiritual life. After hitting the snooze button of life more often that I'd like to admit, I came to realize that cultivating my spiritual life alone was not enough to live fully the abundant life to which Christ calls me. In fits and starts, I slowly began to care better for *all* of myself. My reasons for living a healthier life during this time were mostly personal and practical—better health, lower weight, increased emotional resilience, more energy, an improved sense of well-being, and the ability to keep up with my kids. For too long I took for granted self-care practices like adequate rest, regular exercise, and life-giving play. Over time, I have discovered that these are as vital to holiness and health as are worship and serving others.[6]

Couple that revelation of Dr. Gorman with this research presented by Mark Hayse at the 2012 Association of Youth Ministry Educators:

Seventy-five percent of clergy are overweight or obese . . . one thing is clear: Christian faith does not appear to make a consistent difference in the physical health. In the best light, some research suggests that the incidence of obesity in the church doesn't differ from that found in the general population. At worst, however, much research suggests that *the church may be a contributing factor in the greater incidence of obesity among its leadership and youth.*[7]

In my own journey, I've come to heartily agree with Joe and see the reality of what Mark candidly points out. Shouldn't we be doing better? Youth events notoriously serve food that does not always benefit the body. Being the body of Christ and seeking to follow Jesus speaks to our behavior in all arenas of life. We just often don't have "ears to hear." I'm not my best self when I'm not eating right, getting adequate rest, and regularly doing physical exercise. Being our best selves is part of our worship offering to God, and so caring for my body is critical. And I've experienced the dark side of this reality.

In 2010, I crashed. In my family, that period has become known as my "summer of discontent." It lasted for a year to eighteen months but was the worst in the summer of 2010. Whether it was a midlife crisis, an emotional breakdown, or what, I'm not sure. But the bottom fell out of my life due to a lack of attention to my physical and psychological health. I got to such a dark place that my wife and I wondered if I'd ever be able to step into a classroom or pulpit again.

It was a stressful time. I was completing my doctoral program, attempting to be a good dad and husband, running our denomination's North American youth worker training organization, doing as many side hustles—speaking and writing—as possible to make ends meet besides my full-time gig as professor, turning forty . . . it was a tough period.

All my life seemed to crash to a halt as I experienced extreme insomnia, anxiety, and panic attacks. (I had no idea what a panic attack was until I'd experienced a couple on small planes and didn't understand why I was freaking out.)

If those things were not enough, the worst part was the feeling that God had abandoned me. During that time, I had no sense of God's presence in my life. That contrast revealed to me the reality that I had sensed God for essentially my entire adult life and a good portion of my childhood . . . even though during my teen years I was not following Jesus. Even then, Jesus was seeking me, working in my life.

But during this dark time, the perceived absence of God was the very worst part. I felt an isolation and aloneness I had never felt. That coupled with the insomnia made me feel just wretched. I dreaded each evening. As it began to get dark, my anxiety skyrocketed. I knew I would be awake and alone in our home while my wife and kids slept. I cannot describe the sense of loneliness I felt through night after night of being awake for hour after hour, longing to sleep but not sleeping. The late afternoons and evenings marked a growing sense of fear each day.

Similar to what was experienced by Will Smith's character in the film *I Am Legend*, I felt that each darkening day meant that my entire existence could be threatened due to the enemies that lurked just outside the door. My enemies were not rabid, zombie creatures, however, they were worse because they were in my head.

I sought help from doctors, psychologists, naturopaths, hypnotherapists, acupuncturists, books, spiritual direction, meditation, deep-diaphragmatic breathing, friends, and family. I weekly asked for prayer at church, in my small group, and with friends. I spent hundreds, maybe thousands, of dollars on supplements, natural sleep remedies, and anti-stress herbs; I was open to just about anything that was legal and ethical.

I was contemplating getting a prescription for antianxiety medication my doctor suggested, but when I read the warnings regarding side effects (they are *really* scary, by the way) one of them was . . . wait for it . . . increased anxiety! Seriously? I could take this medication for relief, and it may make it worse? *No thanks!*

Although I wondered if it could actually get any worse, I didn't want to find out. So, I continued to read, research, and seek answers and remedies that were nonpharmaceutical since the pharmaceutical scared me.

In time, all of these efforts slowly—imperceptibly at first—led to healing. Looking back on that time, I can more clearly see what seemed to help the most. While I believe each step I took contributed to the process of healing, a few practices have stuck in the eight-plus years since that period: deep-diaphragmatic breathing, meditation, spiritual direction, and herbal sleep and relaxation remedies.

Before this time, I thought exercise was all I needed to manage stress. I didn't recognize that I was so overdedicated to my workout regime that it became a source of, rather than a tool for, managing stress (fun, eh?). As one naturopath said to me very early in this process, "You seem to have been experiencing a medium to higher grade level of stress for a very long time. If you don't change how you are dealing with that, you will crash."

I didn't think he knew what he was talking about. I should have listened to him. However, my insurance didn't cover my visits to him, so after several visits, I just didn't think we could afford it anymore. I wish I had continued to seek his wisdom.

I share all of this to illustrate the need, in our physical health, to deal not only with our bodies but with our minds as well. We all face stress. Some of us have more, some of us have less. We all experience periods of time that are more stressful than other times. But it seems, more and more, that health professionals are recognizing the extremely damaging effects stress has on our bodies, psyches, and even souls.

Figuring out what works for you is vital. If you've never tried it, I would encourage you to learn about deep breathing. Google it—you'll find information and apps that may help.* I'm convinced that stress-management is a key to longevity, health, and well-being. The two most important parts of my process toward health and wholeness were seeing my spiritual director monthly and deep breathing. I began the practice of deep breathing for as long as I could two or more times per day during the summer of 2010. Sometimes my anxiety was so bad I could only sit down for two or three minutes at a time, and so that's what I did. This practice, however, slowly helped to address my overall stress. Although there is a lot more to that, deep breathing was a means of grace for me.

The other means of grace for me was spiritual direction. I was aware of the art of spiritual direction, which is a practice from the early church of seeking a seasoned Jesus-follower to help us see where and how God may be at work in our lives. I had met with a spiritual director, Trisha, many times before. But I fell out of practice and touch with her. I sought her out and she was the very voice of God to me during this time (and continues to be).

Just to be clear, I do not think she is God, is channeling God, or anything like that. I do think Trisha knows and loves God and me and listens with the ear of her heart to my journey and reflects back to me where and how God *may* be at work in my life. But the discernment process of this is always up to me. I am the final authority in deciding if her insights are accurate. Trisha was the person who said the most devastating and life-giving thing to me during this time: "Mike, all of life is gift."

---

*Insight Timer is a free app that I have found to be helpful in meditation.

When she first said this, I didn't know how to incorporate it into what I was experiencing at that time. How could anxiety, panic, and a sense of God's absence be a gift? Actually, I was angry. However, "Wounds from a friend can be trusted" as the writer reminds us in Proverbs 27:6, and although a bit wounded, I knew I could trust Trisha and I did. I told her during that session that I really didn't know what to do with that, but that I didn't like it. She offered support and her kind, gentle smile . . . and I suspected that she might be right.

In successive sessions she continued that theme: "All of life is gift." Somewhere along the line I started to believe her. That was transformational to recognize the most difficult, painful, and horrible experience of my entire forty years to be reframed as "gift." Although I didn't have eyes to see or ears to hear that fully, I began to accept that it was possible. That possibility grew, in time, to full acceptance and belief, and God has demonstrated again and again the truth of that in my life and journey. I have a deeper sense of empathy, compassion, and tenderness than could have ever been cultivated without that period.

I'd never, never choose to go back and repeat that time, but I have come to believe it was a gift—and part of that gift was experiencing the absence of God. I'm not sure how to put it into words, but I feel a sense of blessing to have walked through my own "dark night of the soul."

Professional Health

I tell my students that the process of interviewing at a church is a lot like dating.[8] Initially, each party tries to put the best foot forward. All the right things are said, each is treated with respect, care, and concern. Essentially, each side of the process is "selling" themselves to the other. Once the job offer is accepted and several months pass, the relationship moves into the marriage stage when each party begins see more of the "real" us. This is good and natural and a great deal more comfortable in time. However, a very important rule of thumb is that if in the course of this dating process the "best behavior" of one of the parties is less than respectful, this should be a warning that the situations will probably only get worse in time.

A few months before I graduated from seminary, I had the pleasure of speaking with several pastors about the potential to join their staffs as the youth pastor. It was a truly enlightening time and not always very encouraging. Some invited me, even urged me, to break the commitment I had with the church I was serving at that time in order to begin my ministry with them while I was still in my master's program. When I suggested that I did not feel good about the idea of doing that, given the deep investment the church (and my supervisor) had made in me, one leader simply told me, "Come on, it's not that big of a deal."

I argued that I had given my word, and I felt that was important. This leader disagreed, and it was the end of our conversation and process. Another pastor led with the amount of money I would be paid, which was attractive for a staff position. But I actually believed the salary was *not* the most important part of this arrangement. I was concerned with the relationships I would have with the lead pastor and the others on staff. However, almost his only talking point was, "You're not going to get an offer of this much money anywhere else."

He was right, by the way, but that was not my only criteria to make this decision. It was weird, frustrating, and a clear sign that the relationship would not be a good fit.

Perhaps the most frustrating interaction I had, however, was with a pastor who was uber-interested in an interview. We began our conversations close to graduation and my impending wedding and seven-week honeymoon on which we would backpack through Italy, Greece, and Turkey. So we agreed the interview would have to wait until my wife and I returned in July. I assured him of my interest, but he wanted more of a commitment from me and asked for my travel schedule, when I would arrive back in the U.S., where I would be staying, and even the phone number of my mother-in-law's house, where we would spend a couple days recovering from jet lag. I thought this was a bit invasive but was also delighted to be pursued so strongly. I shared the requested details with him and asked that he not call on the day we returned, realizing our twenty-hour travel day would leave me tired, likely irritable, and at least a bit loopy. He promised to wait to call, and we agreed to talk about eight weeks from that conversation.

We had a fantastic time abroad but long and tiring return flights from Istanbul. Even less fun was the rush-hour Bay Area traffic we were stuck in from the San Francisco airport to my mother-in-law's house in Walnut Creek. That took nearly two hours, and when we finally got to her house, I found the bed and was falling asleep when she told me there was a phone call for me.

I couldn't imagine anyone calling besides my parents to welcome me back and inquire about our trip . . . but no, it was the pastor who had agreed not to call me. Once I realized what was happening, I was not particularly kind. I asked him if he realized that I had just gotten home and reminded him that I had requested he not call on that day.

He said he had been waiting so long that he wanted to move forward with setting up the interview schedule. I explained to him that I could not imagine working with a person who so blatantly disregarded my boundaries, went back on their word, and could not wait even eighteen more hours to make this connection. I told him in no uncertain terms that our conversation was finished. I was more than a little upset.

The next day, in the light of a new day and twelve hours of rest, I felt clear and centered. When the phone rang, I knew it was him. He apologized, tried to minimize what had occurred, and invited me again to come interview. I calmly reiterated that I was not interested in working with a person who violated a simple request. I explained that if this was the way he treated me during the interview process, I could not imagine how he might violate my boundaries if I were on staff. And that was the end of that.

Another aspect to a person's professional health is to continue to learn. It doesn't matter whether you choose to do this in formal settings through educational institutions, or through less formal settings, such as continuing to read widely and deeply about ministry, culture, and families, or by attending conferences. However, I would argue that any person who is going to serve in ministry for a lifetime should earn a master of divinity degree.

What matters is that you continue to grow, learn, and sharpen your tools (mind). I really like the organization National Network of Youth Ministries (NNYM).[9] It is a great organization whose sole purpose is to connect youth workers, regardless of their denomination, creedal belief, or polity, so they are not alone. And that is a big deal because being a new youth minister can be an isolating experience. Unlike being a new teacher, accountant, social worker, engineer, etc., a new youth minister doesn't necessarily have another person in the building to ask for help about their specific job. Of course you should be able to speak to your lead pastor about such things, but even if they were a youth minister at one time, they aren't currently doing the things on a daily, weekly, and monthly basis that you are. That's the brilliance of the National Network. From their website you can find networking groups in your area so you can connect with other like-minded folks.

Nothing is as potentially deadly for a youth minister as to feel alone. That can erode a person inside and has often, sadly, led to youth ministers making career-ending choices.

In caring for professional health, another part of the conversation involves the way the week is structured. Although everyone's week has 168 hours, not everyone uses those hours strategically and intentionally. It can be helpful to think wisely about how you spend your time each day and to divide those days into a rhythm that makes sense for you and the tasks you need to complete each week.

Although I'm sharing my plan with you, if you try to follow it exactly, it may not work or fit—kind of like David putting on Saul's armor. But it may help you consider how to best leverage your schedule to provide time to focus upon the things you want to focus.

Monday

A wise lead pastor asked why my day off each week was Monday. I really didn't know except that in my first church all of the staff did this. My wise friend suggested I take Fridays off each week. He argued that Mondays are a tough day to have off since many of us in ministry suffer from the Monday Blues—a feeling of letdown following the week's most intense day of service.[10] He felt people who face the Monday Blues shouldn't impose that on their families on their day off.

So Mondays can be a great day to do administrative work in the office—returning calls, clearing out the inbox (email, snail mail, voice mail, etc.), cleaning up the youth room from the weekend events, filling the church van with gas or getting it washed, creating the format for the month's newsletter, or whatever doesn't take a bunch of brain power or creativity but needs to be done. As you clean off your literal and proverbial desktop, you set yourself up to be very productive on Tuesday. It's a great day to fire off the thank you cards you've meant to send, to pray for each kid you are concerned about, or to write postcards to teens you didn't see on Sunday or have not seen for a while—set a goal to write notes to ten kids each Monday. If you do this, before long you'll hear from parents that your "postcard ministry" is really making a difference in their child's life!

Monday is a good day to keep a bit shorter hours, too. Maybe you can come in a little later than normal or go home early—with your supervisor's approval. I recommend not meeting with people on Monday if you're typically worn out after the weekend's activities or doing anything that requires deep thinking or creativity. Don't start working on your speaking materials for the next week! It is also a good day to set appointments for the week with youth, parents, youth workers, or other staff. Generally, Mondays are a great day to get organized.

Tuesday

Now you are set up to have an uber-productive, creative-juices-flowing-because-I'm-rested-and-ready day. The inbox is cleaned out, the desktop is cleared off, and you are ready to walk in and hit it hard for the morning. This provides some separation from the weekend, two nights of rest, and a realization that you can live again.

Tuesday is the perfect day to get to the office early, close your door and send all calls to voice mail, not look at your email, and mute (or better, turn off) your phone and set it aside. It's a perfect day to spend the entire morning being "unavailable" (really set it up with your office personnel, get the okay from your lead pastor and then do it—consistently) to calls, visits, and anything except an emergency. Now, you've just created an incredible block of time—say 8 a.m. to 12 p.m.— to prepare for teaching (reading, research, writing, etc.), work on deep planning (think retreat, twelve-month calendar, the upcoming mission trip, etc.), or focus on other time-demanding activities that simply don't get done in fifteen- and twenty-minute increments.

If you structure your Tuesdays like this, you will have this time to look forward to each week because you can really dig in. I found these blocks of time immeasurably helpful to do the creative work of long-range planning as well as to simply make sure I was ready to teach, speak, and lead that week. The key is to do this consistently and jealously guard these mornings just like you need to jealously guard your day off, vacation time, and evenings when you are scheduled to be home.

After the morning focus time, Tuesday afternoon is a great time to connect with people. Develop relationships with several kids by establishing a standing Tuesday afternoon appointment to shoot hoops or play ultimate Frisbee or shoot some pool or play ping pong right after school for an hour. It's a way to systematically weave relationships into the very rhythm of your work week. It's also an easy way to connect with the friends of youth group kids before a midweek program. If you have administrative help (first, thank Jesus right now that you do!), then a standing Tuesday afternoon meeting with your administrative assistant can be a great way to be sure that any details that need to be promoted that week or gathered for the church website, or other tasks, get covered.

In summary, spend the morning doing important "deep" work and spend the afternoon connecting with people.

I loved my Tuesday mornings as a youth pastor! I often broke them up into sixty- or ninety-minute periods and spent a period reading a book (theology, culture, or other) or commentaries, and then prepared for the week's lessons. I'd spend the last portion doing some calendar/event planning. Since we had established a twelve-month calendar I knew when things were scheduled and coming so I could break up my weeks far enough in advance to do the more detailed planning beyond the date, place, and theme.

Wednesday

This was the day for our church staff meetings, so I planned the entire morning through lunch to be in staff meeting. Your church may meet on a different day or for a shorter period. You'll fit it in however you need to, but plan on it and allow sufficient time for all the other things you need to do as well. The worst thing you can do is to complain about the staff meeting. Since it's consistent (I hope), there is no excuse to not be there on time and prepared. Work around it to accomplish your other tasks.

Since the morning was spent in meeting, I often spent the afternoon preparing for the midweek youth group meeting. Through the afternoon, I would gather any needed items, supplies, game materials or props, and then I would do my best to go spend some time at home, chill, and eat dinner before being back at church by 6:30 p.m. so I could welcome teens and youth workers before 7 p.m.

Thursday

My best suggestion is to use the same schedule on Thursday that you had on Tuesdays. Spend the morning digging in and the afternoon following up with people. Whether it's lunch with a youth worker, coffee with a parent, or having a soda after school with a young person, spend the afternoon connecting with people. If your midweek program takes place earlier in the week, Thursday is a good follow-up day. Or perhaps you need to meet with another staff person at your church to work out some detail from the past or coming up in the future. It's also a great day to make sure you are ready for Sunday so you do not have to return to your office or the church building until Sunday morning. Set up the youth room, run errands (invite kids to join you), and take care of your business so you are free to have a weekend just like "real" people do.

Friday

Friday is your day off. Often I get youth worker pushback on this one because Friday nights are nights for youth activities, or games at the local schools. Yes, that is true. But my standard response is this: Who oversees your calendar? The answer is: You.

There is *no* earthy reason why youth group events should occur on more than one or two Friday nights during the month. If you follow that advice, then you will have two to three Friday nights a month free. Yes, you'll have some that are scheduled, but that isn't a huge deal since you are prepared for Sunday. And while you may not have the entire weekend off, you'll have a complete day off and that's okay occasionally. But be sure you protect that time off. And when you have the weekend retreat, which means you don't have a single day off in seven days, then you need to work out "comp time" (compensation time) with your lead pastor. The idea is simple. You spent your "weekend" working and although it may not be realistic to take Monday and Tuesday off, you should be able to shave down the time you spend in the office the following week to get the rest you need. This is a vital concept given the frequently breakneck speed of ministry with young people. Having the flexibility and trust from your lead pastor is critical to longevity and health.

Saturday

Unless you are traveling with young people or have a planned event, this is a day off (Sabbath).

Sunday

This is a workday. Realize this and explain it to your spouse and family as well. Sundays are not your "Sabbath." They may be everyone else's, but they are not yours. Sundays can be good days for youth worker or parents' meetings to occur right after worship (as long as lunch is included), or for trainings to occur for small-group leaders or for student leaders (if applicable).

It can be very strategic to plan meetings to occur right after a weekly program time since people are already in the building. It's much better than having to come back at another time. Sundays can be a good day for many of these events. Below I have created a block schedule of this plan. I like to call it Plan A because it's the best-case scenario and what should happen most weeks. Like all things, however, sometimes I'm scrambling and have thrown out Plan A, Plan B, and Plan C as well.

This is something I would share with my supervisor and office personnel as well, so they can see how I've planned my week and understand why I'm out most Tuesday and Thursday afternoons. What is not on here is my plan for my own disciplines, such as exercise, sleep, and spiritual formation. You may want to add those as a tool of personal accountability to share with your supervisor. Those times, for me, occur in the early morning hours . . . or they don't occur at all.

Plan A: Visual Representation of the Week

	Monday	Tuesday	Wednesday	Thursday	Friday	Saturday	Sunday
Morning (8-12p)	Arrive Later Admin Day	Arrive Early Study Day!	Staff Mtg	Arrive Early Study Day!	Day Off	Sabbath	Worship, Teach
Afternoon (1p-5p)	Clean Youth Room, Depart Early	Standing Appt Admin	Prepare for Program, Home	Meet with People	Day Off	Sabbath	Mtgs
Evening (6p-10p)	Home	Home	Program	Home	Day Off	Sabbath	Program

Relational Health

Some of the relationally richest time in our lives is spent in weekly and monthly planned activities with friends who became soul friends.

I'll share about a few such experiences in my own life in hopes that it might spark an intentional group in your own life that may bring rich relational health.

One group in my life was a weekly "date night." Every Friday night, four couples brought their kids to one couple's home at 6 p.m. The kids had already been fed and bathed and were in comfortable clothes. Then the schedule from 6 to 7 p.m. was for them to play games or just simply be together. At 7 p.m., typically some organized activity began—often watching a movie. At 8 p.m., it was bedtime. Tooth brushing, etc., commenced and kids were herded into different parts of the house as family groups or by gender or sometimes all together in one room for a big slumber party. Then from 8:15 or so, the kids "slept" while the hosting couple occupied themselves until parents came to pick up their little angels at 10 p.m.

It wasn't unusual for a couple to return early and spend several minutes (or hours) hanging out with the host couple. It became this wonderful weekly practice of spending quality time with our spouses and then monthly, as the hosts, spending time with a wonderful group of kids and sometimes with their parents as well. The relationships that developed between families were rich and a gift to each of us. Not only was it just plain fun to have this to look forward to each week, but also the opportunities to talk were a treat. Some weeks, the three couples who went out met back together by 8:30 or 9:00 for dessert and to play games or just talk. It was a rich relational time. Although it was not a book study or a prayer group, those kinds of interactions, support, and discussions happened organically. Watching each other's kids grow up—and having a small part in that process—was an awesome responsibility and gift.

As the kids got older the routine changed, but the consistent weekly practice did not for many years, in fact. Although not a plan for church growth, date night could certainly provide a great resource to connect with acquaintances and neighbors.

Another monthly practice Sandy and I shared was "dinner club." Dinner club came about almost accidentally as my wife talked with a couple of other women about their love of cooking and eating ethnic food. That casual conversation quickly developed into a plan of action where, monthly, couples met in one of the homes for a family-style meal. Hosting rotated, with the host setting the theme and providing the main course for the evening. Each couple would be assigned or given suggestions for side dishes that would complement the entree.

The very first night of dinner club that Sandy and I hosted, my wife selected Indian food. I remember the smells, tastes, and excitement of that first night. It felt like we were on the verge of something special . . . and little did we know how special that group would become to us for the next ten years! Monthly, eight of us met for a meal from around the world—German, French, Turkish, Southern BBQ, Italian, Indian, Mexican, South American—we tried them all! I don't remember any fails, but I do remember the rich conversations, relationships, and connection of sharing life with these precious people. Our kids were all roughly the same age, so we navigated how to parent kids and, later, how to care for aging parents, together. I'll never forget going through my "summer of discontent." Dinner club was there for me.

These people faithfully prayed for me and supported me like family. Once, I was sitting across a desk from another man in our group. Tearfully, I shared some of the dark details about what I'd been experiencing. When I finished talking, he said nothing—he just cried with me. That demonstration of absolute solidarity and "being with" me was like cold spring water to my parched soul. There was nothing that my friend could have done in that moment that would have meant more. I didn't feel like God was near me at that time, but I came to see the care of others as evidence of God's continuing care even when I didn't feel it.

I've also found a third source of deep connections through the years within the groups of men or individual men I've been regularly connected with. Although I've participated in men's accountability groups, Bible studies, and group spiritual direction for most of my adult life, the connections I've made through my mountain biking, running/hiking, snow, and water skiing "groups" have proven to be long-lasting. It's not so much the specific activity but that a sport provided a common interest and something for us to do together. Men aren't always great at sitting and talking, but put a club, racket, or ball into their hands or a bike or pair of skis under them and the relational boundaries quickly melt away. Some of my deepest friendships have been forged through sweating together on a steep grind up the side of a mountain in the Owyhees on the back of a mountain bike. None of us were great athletes; we just shared a common interest in doing physical stuff and fighting gravity and the middle-age bulge.

Those common interests have led to mountain biking trips, camping, days on the lake and slopes, and many other adventures (like our annual "feats of strength," which is a story for another day). During an activity there is a lot of shared time and space—whether that is sitting on a chair lift, grinding the way up a hill on a bike, sitting in a car on the way to the event or returning home. I have discussed, debated, listened, prayed, cried, laughed so hard I thought something would break, and just lived more fully because of these times. The men I've shared these activities with have all been Christians, but occasionally a man who is not a Christian is invited and quickly sees that our group is unique. While there is a fair bit of trash talk, there is a strong undercurrent of deep love, respect, and support. Often these "outsiders" express a deep admiration for what we all share. Friendships like ours are not common among men, yet they are so very needed if we hope to live in relationships that enable us to embrace all that it means to live on purpose, integrating into the body of Christ and the mission of Christ.

Groups like these provide relational fuel that helps drive our longevity in ministry. Now, twenty years later all spent in the same local church, those relationships sustain Sandy and me. Ministry can be such an isolating experience, which is so ironic—around people all the time but never feeling "known." Intentionally developing regular practices of relational connection with peers is a key to longevity. Whatever form your relational connections take is not what is central, but the fact that you have relational connections is the key.

Spiritual Health

To act like the already discussed "healths" do not contribute to a person's spiritual health creates a false dichotomy and a Greek-like separation of the soul from the body. So, let's not do that. Our health is like a mobile that hangs from the ceiling, and unless all parts are in balance, the mobile will not hang correctly or rotate as it was designed. So, when our relationship quotient is full, when our physical health is being cared for, when we are seeking healthy boundaries at work and in ministry, all these realities contribute to our overall well-being and wholeness.

However, all this doesn't quite go far enough if we do not adapt some intentional practices of cultivating a deeper walk with the Creator. The hazard of ministry is that our time in sermon or lesson preparation can become a substitute for our own personal formation and creating time for reading the Bible for our own growth. We must allow the ancient text to simply wash over us, to simply be present to it and the Spirit without asking something from them. That is, in part, what it means to read the Bible as Scripture. Rather than looking for the historical, literary, contextual meaning as we do in preparing a sermon, we need to regularly come to the Bible and read it so that it more deeply shapes our souls. We allow it to speak however the Spirit chooses to in those moments.

At times in my life, particularly when I was younger, I found it most helpful to participate in small groups for accountability and Bible study. Now, in middle age, I find that accountability happens more organically, and deep and direct questions come from those I hike, bike, ski, or run with weekly. My practices now take place in the early mornings and generally consist of Bible reading (I like the one-year Bible reading plans) and then spending time in silence and prayer. Of course I also participate in a small group that meets on Sunday mornings (some call that Sunday school, but I've heard experts say Sunday school is "dead"—my church hasn't yet received that message) as well as corporate worship, which is the lifeblood of a Christian as we weekly respond to "God's Spirit desire to gather (breathe in) the body of Christ in order to send it out (exhale it) to participate in God's present and coming kingdom."[11]

I *have* to worship regularly with my community of faith. I'm anemic without it. It's not about the style of music, or even the quality of the preaching (although I do care greatly about those things), but it's about gathering with the community to worship, give thanks, share in the sacraments, and give my offering of praise and resources to the one from whom all blessings flow. As John Wesley said, it is a "means of grace" that I need in order to be empowered to live as Jesus in the world. I simply cannot be a Christian without corporate worship. As I like to say, "Christianity is not an individual sport."

Again, it's less about a template or doing the "right things," but regularly doing the things that shape our soul and entire being to be more aligned with the eternal God who knows, loves, and cares for us "as we are, not as we should be"[12] and more than we can comprehend. And, since Christians throughout history have done things like reading the Bible, praying, seeking solitude and silence, taking time to fast, give of themselves and their possessions, feed the hungry, care for the sick, and go on retreats and pilgrimages, then we probably should consider that list as well if we want to truly be integrated into the body of Christ.

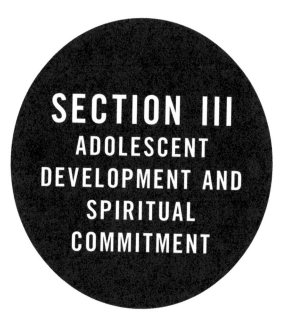

SECTION III
ADOLESCENT DEVELOPMENT AND SPIRITUAL COMMITMENT

This section provides some basic information about the normal development of young people and the reality that various youth are at various stages of openness to the spiritual journey. I've asked Dr. Mindy Coates Smith to provide a primer on the adolescent journey and tasks involved to move toward adulthood. —Michael A. Kipp

I see no hope for the future of our people if they are dependent on the frivolous youth of today, for certainly all youth are reckless beyond words . . . When I was young, we were taught to be discreet and respectful of elders, but the present youth are exceedingly [disrespectful] and impatient of restraint.
—Hesiod, eighth century BC[1]

Young people need models, not critics.
—John Wooden[2]

Rejoice, young person, while you are young! Your heart should make you happy in your prime. Follow your heart's inclinations and whatever your eyes see, but know this: God will call you to account for all of these things.
—Ecclesiastes 11:9, CEB

FOUR

Adolescent Development and Spiritual Formation
by Mindy Coates Smith

● ● ● ● ● ● ● ● ● ● ● ●

History of Adolescent Development

The psychosocial development of adolescents is a relatively new concept to explore. The term "psychosocial" refers to the psychological development of a person within the scope of their social environment.

We must first define what we currently mean by "adolescence." The term is somewhat of a new notion, gaining momentum and credibility as a legitimate phase of the life span in the last hundred years. Psychologist G. Stanley Hall introduced the idea of adolescence and depicted his thoughts on the issue in his 1904 work, *Adolescence.* He described adolescence as a "new birth" replicating an ancient period of "storm and stress" when the old gets broken down in order to welcome the new.[1]

This allowed a grouping to form for young people caught between the two categories of childhood and adulthood. By the beginning of the twentieth century, the stage of adolescence was generally accepted as a justifiable phase of the life span and began to develop its own subculture.[2]

A noteworthy psychoanalyst on the topic of human development was Margaret Mahler, a Hungarian physician who took an interest in child development and advanced the separation-individuation theory of attachment. The separation-individuation process takes place between approximately the fifth month of life until the thirty-sixth month and is a period that involves the child's achievement of separate functioning with the emotional support of the mother.[3] This phase allowed for the separation from the child's role of infant to the role of toddler.

In a similar fashion, German psychoanalyst Peter Blos applied Mahler's theory to another stage of human development, calling it the second individuation phase. In this process, the child renegotiates the separation-individuation issue at the beginning of the adolescent journey, allowing for the separation from the role of child to the role of adolescent.[4]

But when does this adolescent journey begin? Most experts agree that the onset of adolescence begins with the arrival of puberty, measured by the average age of the onset of female menses.[5] This is beginning at a younger age, with ten percent of U.S. girls menstruating before eleven years of age.[6]

Even though the onset of adolescence is generally defined by physiological changes, the psychological adjustments and sociological modifications accompany this process at the same time.[7] Therefore, the transition from the role of child to the role of adolescent is beginning at a younger age, shortening the era of childhood and lengthening the period of adolescence.

The end of adolescence is much more ambivalent as it depends on cultural markers into adulthood that can last until the mid to late twenties. Because of the length of the adolescent journey, experts have divided adolescence into early, mid, and late stages of the individuation process.[8] These substages are becoming even more nuanced as more research is done in the pockets of these differing phases. For example, the late adolescent journey into adulthood has been deemed by some experts as emerging adulthood, almost placing a new developmental phase between adolescence and adulthood.[9]

In the past, human development has been understood, or defined, by the progression of the individual through differing developmental stages. This idea stems from the work of developmental theorist Jean Piaget, specifically his theory of cognitive development. The basic premise of Piaget's work was that cognitive development is formed from the construction of increasingly sophisticated forms of logic, beginning with sensorimotor skills (birth to age two), moving to preoperational (ages two to seven), then to concrete operational (ages seven to eleven), and finally to formal operational (age eleven and older).[10]

This fundamental idea of developmental growth through stages strongly influenced mid-century psychoanalyst Erik Erikson. Erikson designed an eight-stage theory of psychosocial development in which each stage presented a conflict that served as a turning point based on the ego strength of the individual.[11]

During adolescence, Erikson argued, the individual must experience and endure a crisis of identity in order to overcome inner and outer struggles.[12] The success of this process somewhat depends on the cultural relativity and social norms of the situation in which the individual confronts each conflict. In this way, Erikson's definition of the adolescent journey is largely based on identity formation. Swiss psychiatrist Carl Jung defines the process of adolescence as individuation and differentiation,[13] while scholar James Loder describes it as becoming one's own person.[14] These definitions summarize the tasks of adolescence as identity formation, accepting responsibility for life choices, and finding a place to belong (in short, identity, autonomy, and belonging).[15]

Environmental Factors

As the individual navigates the adolescent journey with these three tasks at hand, several influencing factors are along the way. Perhaps one of the most significant is what psychologists call the environment, meaning the social context in which the individual lives, including culture, education, and relationships. Individuals who share the same social environment are assumed to have similar experiences and points of view. This is closely related to the nature vs. nurture debate, which has left psychologists divided over which of these two factors has more influence on individual behaviors over time.[16]

Noteworthy psychologist Kurt Lewin proposed that both nature *and* nurture interact to shape the individual and that the ever-evolving process of interaction is the best way to understand behaviors.[17] Therefore, it seems appropriate to reason that, when evaluating the behaviors of individuals within the same general social context, the influences of the environment should be considered, along with the individual interaction within this context. This is what researchers mean by the psychosocial aspect of development.

The psychosocial development of the adolescent closely intertwines with spiritual development since the quest for identity, autonomy, and belonging continues to drive choices made during this time of life, including those associated with spirituality. Some scholars suggest that because of the many physiological changes during puberty, there is a close relationship to the emergence of sexuality, love, and religious experience.[18] Other research indicates that adolescents experiencing developmental transitions (especially during early and late adolescence) are more vulnerable to their interaction with society in how these situations predict their decisions and behaviors.[19] This suggests that outside influences of the environment can affect the way adolescents make decisions, even about spiritual matters.

Contemporary Theories of Adolescent Development

It is helpful to have a basic understanding of a few theories to provide a landscape of the various perspectives: the myth of adolescence theory, thriving theory, and abandonment theory.

The myth of adolescence theory is the idea that adolescence is merely a social conjecture and is seriously flawed. Given that the concept of adolescence is relatively new, myth of adolescence theorists predicate that the wisdom of previous centuries should be trusted and that responsibility should be given to people around the age of twelve or thirteen.

In Christian circles, many who have this perspective rely on Dr. David Alan Black and his 1999 work *The Myth of Adolescence: Raising Responsible Children in an Irresponsible Society.* Dr. Black uses the absence of biblical evidence on the topic of adolescence as reason enough to discount this contemporary notion. He promotes the idea of giving responsibility to young people and uses several passages from the Bible to defeat the secularized concept of adolescence.[20]

More recently, in 2007, Dr. Robert Epstein, former editor-in-chief of *Psychology Today,* published *The Case Against Adolescence: Rediscovering the Adult in Every Teen.* Epstein showed that teen turmoil is caused by outmoded systems put into place a century ago, which destroyed the continuum between childhood and adulthood.[21] According to Epstein, where this continuum still exists in other countries, there is no adolescence.

Isolated from adults, American teens learn everything they know from their media-dominated peers, the last people on earth they should be learning from. Epstein explains that teens are highly capable—in some ways more capable than adults—and argues against infantilizing young people.[22] Epstein recommends giving young people adult authority and responsibility as soon as they demonstrate readiness.

Another theory to explore in contemporary adolescent development is the thriving theory, also known as positive youth development. Instead of finding what is wrong with youth, this theory focuses on what is right. According to the U.S. Department of Health and Human Services, "The Positive Youth Development approach understands that all young people need support, guidance, and opportunities during adolescence. It also looks toward creating supportive communities for all young people and at the same time, engaging youth to contribute to the well-being of the larger community."[23]

Positive youth development also emphasizes that youth are producers of their own growth, especially given the human capacity for motivation that drives development.[24]

Finally, a third theory to consider is abandonment theory. This idea stems from the many contributing factors to the complication of the adolescent journey, including a culture of hurriedness, greater levels of stress and anxiety, and a society of abandonment. A landmark book on the rushed timetable children and adolescents face is *The Hurried Child* by David Elkind. The author contends that children are pressured to grow up "too fast, too soon" given the demands of early academic achievement, unrealistic expectations from parents, and premature media portrayals of children in grown-up situations. These burdens create unnecessary stress through responsibility overload, emotional strain, and anxiety due to change.[25]

The onset of many modern conveniences such as microwaves, computers, and cable television have sped up daily life. The introduction of the nanosecond (a billionth of a second) has been brought into the current culture and is a faster unit than the human nervous system is designed to understand.[26] Yet, technology prompts people, including adolescents, to respond to the demands of the nanosecond contributing to today's rushed culture. Those who are hurried during childhood may not understand the hurrying of their lives until they enter adolescence, when they can become resentful and angry.[27]

Dr. Chap Clark takes this notion a step further in his groundbreaking book *Hurt: Inside the World of Today's Teenagers* by labeling the current state of the adolescent as "abandoned." He contends that external systems, such as the classroom or athletics, and internal systems, like safe relationships or intimate settings, have abandoned adolescents by creating a distance between adults and kids and by maintaining organizational structures that are adult-focused.

This lack of support during a crucial time of development has created a culture of isolation for adolescents in which they have no choice but to create their own world beneath the surface.[28] This "world beneath," as Clark describes it, is a complicated culture involving several layers of different egocentric identities that are designed to adapt to adult expectations as needed. This world is lonely and protected by only a few friends to whom the adolescent can cling as they search for individuality, belonging, and legitimacy.

Spiritual Formation of Adolescents

Understanding the psychosocial development of adolescents provides a framework for us to gain insight in the spiritual formation of adolescents, as these are intertwined. In today's context, there is really no complete way to characterize spirituality, especially for the adolescent. In the 2001 publication of *Teen People Faith: Stories of Belief and Spirituality*, the writers introduce the testimonies of various faith journeys with a description of what spirituality is:

Spirituality takes many forms. For some, this means belief in a higher power; for others spirituality means taking a walk in the woods. Whatever their definitions of faith, their stories prove that spirituality is not only a topic worthy of exploration, but an essential part of who we are.[29]

Ultimately, spirituality has become a pluralistic melting pot based on the individual's ideology of what feels best to believe in depending on current circumstances and influences. Despite this ambiguity, authors continue trying to place boundaries on what spirituality is, such as theologian Alister McGrath, who offers that spirituality is "a quest for the fulfilled and authentic religious life, the bringing together of the ideas distinctive of that religion and the whole experience of living on the basis of and within the scope of that religion."[30]

From the perspective of the Christian faith, spirituality describes the "relationship, union, and conformity with God that a Christian experiences through his or her reception of the grace of God, and a corresponding willingness to turn from sin."[31] This description implores a more practical route in which to understand Christian spirituality.

In *The Spirit of the Disciplines*, Dallas Willard suggests that living as Jesus did, like participating in similar activities, such as prayer or study of the Bible, is the way Christians can become most like Christ.[32] This suggests a practical approach of making long-term lifestyle changes so new habits can be formed. This type of responsibility seems difficult to incorporate into the life of an active adolescent who may still be deciding if Christian spirituality will be a lasting piece of their life. Yet at the same time, it does not seem appropriate to deem the commitments of Christian spirituality as too far reaching for the adolescent. Church youth programs, parachurch organizations, and Christian schools have all attempted to translate elements of the Christian life into age-appropriate programs.

However, when addressing the issue of spiritual development, especially concerning adolescents, organized religion is sometimes seen as the enemy of spirituality. "Where religion is regarded as controlling, prescriptive, narrow-minded and ultimately damaging, spirituality is life-giving, nurturing and personally empowering."[33] This creates a tension for Christian organizations, including the church and Christian schools.

Perhaps a way to bridge this gap is to connect some of the alluring components of spirituality with tenets of the Christian faith, such as community, discipleship, and adoption. For the adolescent, community, specifically in peer relations, is one of the most crucial parts of development. This, coupled with the strong influences of community motifs in the Bible (not only with the people of Israel in the Old Testament but also with the invasion of Christ into the human community in the New Testament), makes the theme of community a worthy part of the adolescent journey of Christian spirituality. Discipleship is also an important matter, in which spirituality is practiced as a self-discovery of personhood through Christ by participating in traditions of worship and giving to others' needs.[34] Finally, adoption into the body of Christ speaks to the spiritual need of participating in a greater narrative, or being part of something greater than ourselves.

FIVE
Taking the Next Faithful Step
What Does This Look Like?

● ● ● ● ● ● ● ● ● ● ● ● ●

THE SPRING AND SUMMER after I dropped out of my first year of college, I got a job cutting firewood. Actually, I was *splitting* large tree rounds into firewood. My boss, Carl, a seasoned tree-faller, identified and cut down diseased black oak trees in the national forest. It was an amazing forest-office to go to every day at 4:30 a.m. Carl then proceeded with his impressively hefty, loud, and commanding chainsaw to "limb" the trees—removing the multitude of "arms" that had grown from the giant oak he just felled.

Black oaks are an amazing species of hardwood. They grow all over the western United States from the middle of Oregon to Baja California.[1] A mature black oak can be up to 110 feet tall and 9 feet in diameter![2] When Carl finished limbing the tree, what remained was a very large—often 4- to 5-foot diameter—trunk that was 40 to 60 feet long. He then cut this trunk into sections of about 18 to 24 inches, depending on what the customer wanted.

My job was to turn these sections (or rounds) upright and split them into pie pieces. Then we would load the pieces onto Carl's two-ton, 1958 Ford and deliver them to the customers' homes. We cut two cords a day, five days a week, and I did this job for about six months.

I'll never forget the first day I showed up for work with Carl. I had no idea what to expect; I just needed a job, and a friend had set me up to work with Carl. He said I'd be paid in cash each day. That sounded great! The first thing Carl asked was if I smoked. I said no, and he muttered something to the effect that I should do okay.

I didn't understand what he meant until he showed me the maul that I would use to split the large rounds of "green" (wet) black oak. He demonstrated how to swing the sixteen-pound maul. It looked so easy! He moved so efficiently that, after about ten to twelve smooth swings of that implement, the round of wood was reduced to seven or eight nearly perfectly divided pieces of black oak firewood. Now it was my turn. I picked up the maul—admittedly I felt pretty cocky as a former track and field athlete—and proceeded to swing that thing about 190 times without the wood so much as looking hurt!

I couldn't believe it! I was out of breath (that was what smoking had to do with it), sweating, and more than a little embarrassed. Carl then taught me to "read the wood."

With time, I got better and became much more efficient in my movements. I was never as good as Carl (did I mention I was more than twenty years younger than he was?) but I learned that most rounds just had to be read well, hit a lot, and eventually a crack would develop that would split and then, eventually, we'd have firewood.

I've since reflected on the investment of energy into those rounds to make firewood, and I see a close parallel to (youth) ministry. Not unlike those green-wet rounds, young people are at various points of openness to not only a relationship with a caring, committed, Christian adult but also to taking the next step in their spiritual life.

Doug Fields, in his book *Purpose-Driven Youth Ministry*,[3] talks about the Circles of Commitment and helps the reader to see that different people are at different places of openness to a growing awareness and relationship with Jesus Christ. Although that may be obvious when reflected upon, it is not how youth groups (and even church congregations) are often treated. That is why Fields (and Rick Warren before him) argues that a balanced approach to ministry involves outreach (evangelism[4]), corporate worship, authentic fellowship, growing experiences of discipleship, and opportunities to invest in ministry—and the cycle continues by those people then reaching others.

No youth group (or church) is monolithic. Naturally, different people have different levels of maturity or commitment in their relationship, awareness, or openness to Jesus Christ. Providing opportunities for these various levels of commitment to engage with the body of Christ is imperative.

Some teens in a youth group only want to come for the fun events. They are interested in the church only if they have a chance to play paintball or go skiing. This is generally the largest group of young people in each community. A smaller group of teens is ready to experience various spiritual disciplines. They want opportunities to fast, experience silence, take contemplative walks, or even go on some type of pilgrimage. These teens need occasions to experiment with these classic spiritual disciplines in order to take their next faith step.

So, are we inviting them into these experiences and providing opportunities for them to try out these disciplines—or are we only sponsoring paintball nights and ski trips?

The more serious the level of commitment, the smaller the group will be that is interested. This concept is not unlike a funnel (Figure 2) where the deeper the commitment level the smaller the group of people interested (adults are no different, by the way). The further down the funnel a person goes, the more mature is their commitment to Christ— at least that is the theoretical idea.

Before you tar and feather me for using a marketing funnel to talk about spiritual maturity or commitment, please see how this model does help us to see the youth group as a collection of individuals each with their different spiritual depths or maturity, and even openness to deeper faith response. Of course, models are simplified ways of understanding more complex issues. It is far from perfect, but perhaps it will communicate the two important truths that I did not understand early in my youth ministry career: (1) More people are willing to do the more "fun" stuff, and (2) Just because the whole youth group doesn't want to join our discipleship experiences does not mean we should not plan them.

Figure 2

It was years before I understood this. As a result, I planned a lot of fun stuff and got discouraged when few young people expressed interest in my early morning Bible study or the discipleship retreat. Although basic for some, this is vital to grasp if your youth ministry is going to integrate young people into the body of Christ and the mission of Christ.

So we begin with understanding that young people (adolescents) are at various levels of openness to spiritual things, and then we build our youth ministry calendar to provide opportunities for each level. And just as the number of young people who are interested in activities are toward the top of the funnel, our programming should reflect that same ratio with more activities and events that are attractive to the whole group and less to those further down the road.

Yet here is where the magic is . . . the point of the deeper activities and connecting with those kids does not end with the end of the program or retreat, but it begins with learning who those teens are and then connecting them with others, including caring, committed, Christian adults who will journey with them. The big idea is not to provide religious goods and services for various consumers but to provide opportunities for the next step so young people and old people can come together at various points and continue—together—in their journeys. While I'm not a fan of an attractional ministry model where folks have to come to the church building to receive the message of salvation, I am a fan of the body and bride of Christ and am convinced that a Christian *needs* to be a regular part of the church for their faith to be all that Christ has designed it to be. Christianity is not an individual sport, and there is no such thing as secret-agent Christians.

I'll never forget the incident that brought these truths into focus for me. During one typical night of youth group, I had just completed announcements for the coming week. I was urging the teens to bring friends to nearly every activity planned for the coming week. The group then transitioned to playing a group game. As they moved from their seats, a spiritually mature young woman approached me. She pointed out how I had talked about each event as important enough for them to bring friends. She asked about one specific event and asked if I thought it may be more important than the others. I didn't know how to respond. She suggested it was probably more important for *some* of the kids in the group to attend since it involved a deeper level of spiritual maturity—it was a before-school Bible study that took place each Thursday morning.

Before I could say anything, she added, "When *everything* is important, then *nothing* is important. You may want to think about that when giving the announcements."

Ouch! She was right. Suddenly I became aware of the various levels of spiritual maturity present in the room that night. I was a bit embarrassed by that conversation. (Who likes getting schooled by a high school junior? It's happened a lot over the years, though!) But I was thankful for it. I began to be more honest about the purpose of our planned events and telling teens, "You may not want to come to this unless you enjoy _____." Fill in the blank with silence, spiritual disciplines, messy games, or yard work.

Recognizing that not all events on the calendar appeal to all the kids is vital if we will invite young people to take the next step in their spiritual journey.

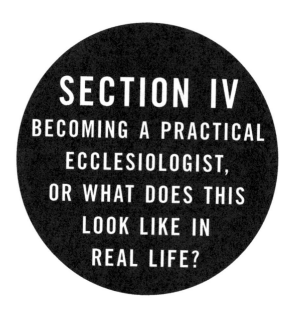

SECTION IV
BECOMING A PRACTICAL ECCLESIOLOGIST, OR WHAT DOES THIS LOOK LIKE IN REAL LIFE?

The greater the supply of religiously grounded relationships, activities, programs, opportunities, and challenges available to teenagers . . . the more likely teenagers will be religiously engaged and invested.
—National Study of Youth and Religion[1]

Youth Ministry is the church's ministry, not just that of specialists who can "relate" to young people. The mandate to be there for young people belongs to the Christian community, not to any individual or group of individuals.
—Kenda Dean[2]

Integration into the body of Christ means helping the entire congregation recognize its role in raising up a child in the faith—a vow we make at an infant's baptism and one we take rather seriously in the case of young children but routinely abandon to "youth leaders" come adolescence.

—*The Godbearing Life*[3]

The aim of youth ministry should be to embed youth in a community of faith that nurtures a maturing faith in Christ.

—Sharon Galgay Ketcham[4]

SIX
Making Room

● ● ● ● ● ● ● ● ● ● ● ●

IT IS EASY TO TALK about integrating young people into the body of Christ, but how do we do that? To be frank, it is about repenting of our programmatic approaches to ministry with young people and then reshaping them to be more relational for the long term. As Kenda Dean and Ron Foster quip in their youth ministry classic, *The Godbearing Life*:

> The indictment to which contemporary youth ministry is vulnerable is careless handling of the soul. We have related to youth admirably; we play catch exceptionally well. But . . . we have failed to enlist them in the missionary movement of Jesus Christ.[1]

But to be enlisted in this movement they must be rightly related to adults who have learned to navigate these countercultural waters. They must be enabled to see what this looks like outside the confines of the youth room or among their peers. They must become integrated into the body of Christ to "feel" their role as a part of that celestial body that is working to make it "on earth as it is in heaven."

Youth Workers

The first layer of this integration strategy begins with the people teaching classes or leading small groups, going on retreats with teens, and interacting with them on a weekly basis. The volunteers you have working with young people are crucial. They must be caring (genuinely loving young people), committed (meaning they show up consistently, not occasionally), and of course Christian (loving Jesus, loving others with a life that reflects that). In fact, Andrew Root argues, "The youth pastor's job is to go to adults within the congregation and invite them to become a place-sharer to an adolescent."[2] He describes a "place-sharer" as someone who "opens their own person to the person of the adolescent."[3]

Clearly, this is much more than simply helping lead games in a midweek program or serving as crowd control. This is about deep, vulnerable, trusting relationship that transforms each person. In view of the challenges of finding adult volunteers to work with the youth, I realize that we are often happy to take whoever is willing. However, this is not what is best for the young people or for the kingdom, and is prone to create more problems than it solves. It's important to have high standards for volunteers and expect their lives to reflect integrity and genuine fondness for young people. And it's worth the time it takes to get the right people into the right places. Firing a volunteer is tough!

The summer before I became the youth pastor at a new church, I learned about an interaction between a volunteer youth worker and the outgoing youth pastor. The group was returning from an international mission experience, and in the middle of being exhausted from ten days of traveling and working in hot, difficult conditions, something went wrong in the travel arrangements.

As the youth pastor shared this news with the group between flights, the volunteer (also the mom of two kids on the trip) went ballistic! She shouted at the youth pastor that it was all his fault, even though the airline had changed the schedule. Not only did she act in a completely unfitting way to the news, but her language was also peppered with profanity. Do you see the weight of this? An adult volunteer was cursing out the youth pastor while they were sitting in an airport in front of the youth group and everyone else who happened to walk by. Great way to end a mission trip.

The worst part? She was still a volunteer when I arrived at the church! I inherited her misdeeds. She was the second volunteer I had to "fire." It wasn't that difficult once I found out about the airport incident and that fact that she was actually stealing from our church café.

It's worth the work to get the right people in the right places. Not doing so can lead to some pretty ugly incidents.

Each adult volunteer or youth worker should have: a job description, *one* weekly responsibility (in terms of the youth ministry program), and the expectation that they will, in time, serve as *pastor* to a small group of young people.

A job description is a key component to clearly communicate the expectations you have for youth workers. A results-oriented job description is so vital that Mark DeVries posits that "everyone from the lead youth staff to the van drivers" must have one (along with an annual review and revision of those documents).[4] The description must communicate the role volunteers play in the larger context of the youth ministry. The description should tell exactly what they are supposed to be doing in the weekly program and throughout the week, and why it matters. Setting expectations from the beginning is central to success and clarity. By clearly outlining what you are and are not asking of them is a gift.

Here are some matters that may be helpful to address:

- First and foremost, they are expected to maintain a healthy relationship with God, Christ's church, and friends outside the youth ministry.
- Their on-time attendance at each weekly program is expected.
- They are expected to be prepared for whatever they may have volunteered (or been *voluntold*) to do that week (such as leading singing or giving a devotional thought or guiding meditation during prayer time). Their preparation matters! After all, this is *their* ministry.
- It is helpful to instruct them to seek out their focus group kids (more about this below) and to sit with them while modeling the

kind of behavior we hope kids will emulate during the program time. When new kids come to a program, invite focus group teens to include them . . . or include them yourself.

- Suggest that they stay connected with their focus group kids during the week by sending them a text or other contact through social media. (Postcards are also something kids love to get. Who gets personal mail anymore?)

- Finally, and perhaps *most* importantly, seek ways to connect these young people to other church members. For example, when hosting a Super Bowl party with peers, youth workers could invite focus group kids to attend as well. What a great and nonthreatening way to grow the circle of care in the lives of a young person.

- They are *not* expected to solve all the problems a young person may face, lend them money, or act as the junior Holy Spirit in the person's life, but to be an adult friend who is available and ready to listen and share.

If we are going to make room for young people and truly integrate them into the body of Christ, that will happen through relationships. These relationships must be intentional circles of care, and one circle is not enough. Young people need to experience intentional concentric circles of committed Christian adults who demonstrate consistent care in their lives. The goal of these relationships is to be a *relationship* that reaches beyond the youth group years.

The next level of care should happen through a weekly small group, Bible study, or fellowship group—whatever the main meeting is for your youth ministry and where new attenders are most likely to come. This can serve as a great place for relationships to be created, maintained, and deepened over time.

This care can happen even if those smaller groups are not explicitly formed, but simply a way of organizing a large group into smaller units. For example, some youth ministries help each volunteer develop a focus group of young people. This becomes the primary focal point of a volunteer's relational ministry. Those are the kids a volunteer specifically looks to connect with when they show up to the weekly program, sitting with these youth and spending time with them, catching up from the previous week. They are also the young people that adult volunteer prays for and sends texts and postcards to.

When you give the volunteer a single program to participate in each week and help them develop a focus group of young people, that's a way to break down being a "volunteer" into a digestible chunk.

A relationship with a nonparental adult is a key aspect that influences a young person to ongoing participation in the faith community.[5] The way a person gets connected will always come through a relationship. By taking an intentional approach to connecting youth and youth workers on the most basic level, we start right in seeking to provide meaningful ministry for adults and meaningful relationships of care for young people.

Another concentric circle of care comes through a follow-up system that systematically tracks each young person's attendance. Whether through a sophisticated technological system involving membership cards and a retina scan or just a paper system of writing down who attended each program, knowing who is coming and who is not coming is a critical part of providing a caring environment and connecting a person to the body of Christ. Once a master list is developed of regular youth group attendees, then a meaningful follow-up system can be implemented. This list becomes your youth ministry directory, and maintaining accurate, up-to-date information is mission critical in integrating young people into the body of Christ. Whatever method (electronic, app based, paper based) works for your context is not particularly important. That the information is gathered, revised, and used to keep in contact with teens is![6]

Once this directory is established, determine what intervals of absence will trigger what kind of response. For example, since most people view "regular attendance" at church to be one to three times per month, maybe it isn't vital to follow up for a person who has come most of the last month to your midweek youth group. However, the volunteer who has that young person in their focus group will probably be in touch with them each week through a quick text or other form of social media contact. If a person misses two or three weeks in a row, however, does that warrant a more involved response? Perhaps a phone call or even a visit?

Each of these steps is certainly contextual, depending on the culture of the youth group, church, and community. But what is not optional is the importance of good follow-up to demonstrate that you care about youth and notice when they are not there. We have all heard heartbreaking stories of people who faithfully attended a church for years and then simply stopped coming—and never heard a word from anyone. What does that communicate to a person? Certainly that they were not "integrated" or important.

Bottom line: track attendance at all weekly activities and then create benchmarks and responses of care when a young person misses x number of sessions. This will show that they are wanted, cared about, and important.

The third level of care is through the youth ministry team connecting young people to adults outside the youth ministry. In *Growing Young* by the great folks at the Fuller Youth Institute, this is called "prioritizing young people (and families) everywhere."[7] This characteristic is the linchpin in their "growing young wheel" that captures the six strategies of churches that are not stagnating but are actually engaging young people fifteen to twenty-nine years old.[8]

A part of this involves finding places of ministry and service (and thus connection and belonging) for young people. Does a young person love computers, sound equipment, and tech? Get them involved with the adults on the tech team. Does a young person have musical gifts? Help that one find a place of regular rotation on the worship team. Does a youth have dreams of being a leader? Help them to find a place of leadership within the church.

Growing Young simply calls this a "load bearing role."[9] Young people need to be given a job that actually matters and is not just busywork. Who wants to simply be in a meaningless and unneeded role? We cannot think of teenagers as "less than" rather than simply "younger than."

"To treat adolescents as a separate species instead of as less experienced members of our own was one of the twentieth century's largest category errors."[10] For young people to become integral to the body, the congregation and the leadership must include young people by giving them not only a voice but also a place to serve—and yes, even, to fail. If they are not relied upon to come through, then are they really a part of the body?

Youth minsters are busy . . . and we can get so caught up in doing the things that are urgent (preparing this week's lesson or post-football-game activity) that we push what is important to the back burner. Although that is a reality, at times, too often it becomes the pattern we follow perennially. This can perpetuate the dropout problem after a young person graduates from the youth group. We have failed them by failing to facilitate relationships with adults outside the youth ministry.

Clearly, not all young people will want this kind of connection. That's okay. But for those who do, it can be transformative, and it helps the church to be what God has designed it to be—an intergenerational community demonstrating a better way to live.

In the beginning of this book there was a blog entry from Kevin, who was a youth group member many years ago. He was an aspiring teacher/preacher/leader and expressed a desire to help with the children's ministry. The adult volunteer who weekly shepherded Kevin caught wind of this, brought it to the youth pastor's attention, and a meeting was set up with the children's director to see where Kevin might fit. Within a couple of weeks Kevin was a regular part of a fourth-grade class. That continued for the rest of his sophomore year of high school. By his junior year, Kevin was teaching that class on a rotating basis. During his senior year, Kevin became the primary teacher. He was so consistent and committed that the children's pastor hired him as an intern during his college years.

Kevin received his call to ministry through that experience and, *just* as importantly, Kevin experienced a connection to the church through the ministry with children. Kevin's ministry introduced other adults into his life who counted on him, cared for him, and entrusted him to be a partner in caring for others. Although Kevin may be an exceptional case, perhaps he shouldn't be. If we don't have a pattern of facilitating these kinds of connections within the body, how many Kevins will never have the opportunity to experience this kind of deep, soul-shaping connection?

As Dean and Foster point out, we cannot ignite the flame of faith (let alone a "call to ministry"); that is something only the Holy Spirit can do. But we can create the conditions to burn. In placing the Kevins in previously untried places and with trusted partners, we clear dry ground, place tinder in a pile, and pray for the flame of faith to rise.[11]

What about the young people who aren't interested in teaching a class or serving Communion or even taking the offering? How do we intentionally and systematically present opportunities for them to connect with adults outside the youth ministry? I believe this is limited only by our imagination. Is the youth ministry essentially an entertainment enterprise or is it a way to provide life-giving relationships with people of all ages in a caring community.

Here are three concrete ideas that churches have successfully used to do just that!

1. Story Sunday

Certainly, the easiest of these suggestions to organize, Story Sunday—or whatever day you choose—is simply a designated time, perhaps monthly. The idea here is that during the "teaching time" of the meeting an older person or couple comes and shares their faith journey with the youth group.

It's important to vet who will do this well, but it is a relatively low-threat way for young and old to be together and for the youth to get to know more about people in their congregation. Allowing for questions after the story time adds to the relational connections. Serve some food and you've just created a party to celebrate these new friendships! Numerous benefits come from this simple idea. Youth now "know" an older person and can say hello when their paths cross (of course, they may not take that step, but simply the recognition that "I know that person" can be valuable).

The older people feel honored by the opportunity. They discover the youth group is really a wonderful, caring, and respectful group of teens, and they become a fan of the youth director and kids. Everyone learns that God is at work through all kinds of stories, and the implication is that maybe God could be at work in my story, too. Low threat, fun, and can lead to baby steps of the congregation being more unified.

2. Prayer Partners

Some faith communities have found this to be a very successful way to connect younger and older people in another nonthreatening but slightly more logistically complicated way. Each young person who wants, has their picture taken and fills out a simple form that provides their name, birthday, email, favorite candy, a "bit about me," and a few prayer requests for the school year, or whatever you find helpful.

These pictures are attached to that information form and those in the congregation receive an opportunity to "adopt" a prayer partner for the school year. A good time to present these would be at the beginning of the school year when the congregation could focus on pastoral prayer for "students" of all ages. After the service or during prayer time, the "adoption" forms could be available. Keep records of who adopted whom for follow-up through the year.

The big idea is simply for this form and picture to be placed on the refrigerator or someplace where the adult will see it and remember to daily pray for this young person. That is all that is required except for sending a birthday card, which could be brokered through the youth minister, or small gifts or notes of encouragement throughout the year.

I'll never forget the experience Jack had when we first tried this experiment. Jack was from a nominal Christian home and came to church occasionally. When he did, he was gregarious, often challenged authority, and was disruptive to whatever was taking place (you know the type). Jack had a special place in my heart.

One week Jack came in late to the Sunday morning youth gathering and was walking through the church atrium on the way to the youth room. His prayer partner spotted him and called out, "Hi, Jack! How are you today? I've been praying for you. I hope you know you are loved by God, this church, and me."

She continued to where she was headed. Jack freaked out! He had no idea how this older widow knew his name. He was sure she was some sort of spy working with law enforcement and that she was investigating him. Jack had a guilty conscience—and a habit of smoking marijuana and drinking. He was sure she was on to him.

By the time he reached me in the youth room he was panicking. He took me aside and expressed his discomfort with a fair share of expletives. He stared spouting about how she was likely working with law enforcement and that he would probably be arrested after church. I had no idea what he was talking about. I asked him what this woman looked like and approximately how old she was. When he explained she was a "grandma" type I almost laughed. I reminded him of our efforts to connect youth group members to other adults in our church for prayer and support. Jack's face slowly changed as he digested this information. I asked if he remembered the picture I had taken of him and the form he'd filled out. I suggested that the person in the atrium was most likely Mabel, his prayer partner, and that she probably knew his face because she had been praying for him and looking at his picture on her refrigerator. Jack smiled a mischievous smile and said, "Oh, really? . . . I guess that's kind of cool," and then walked away to connect with his peers.

For a meaningful conclusion to the prayer partners program, in the spring, a luncheon immediately following the worship service could be an excellent time to connect the youth and adults over a simple meal. Assign seats so adults sit with their designated teens. Having a mix of adults and young people at any given table will further provide opportunities for "cross-pollination" of relationships. To avoid awkwardness and facilitate communication, provide some "table talk" cards, or the luncheon host can provide some guided questions for tables to discuss.

The big idea of this gathering is to provide a structured time at church (and thus to avoid any concerns or need for background checks, etc.) for the praying and prayed-for to officially meet. Of course, even better would be to do bookend luncheons—at the beginning of the school year and at the end. But any effort to intentionally connect young and old in structured and thoughtful ways is a step in the right direction. Even better, let each person provide a picture and information form so they can truly be prayer partners. However, that may be more than your church is ready for, and getting started with any type of intentional connection can help.

The presupposition here, of course, is that the adults are more spiritually mature than the young people. At times they aren't, and the teens may suggest that they want a reminder card in order to pray for the adult who is praying for them . . . bravo! That would be the most wonderful response and hopefully one that will come in time.

All youth may not be "adopted" at first. Don't be discouraged. Anytime you try something new, it takes a community time to adjust, particularly if you have not tried this kind of intentional integration before. The youth minister may need to approach adults in classes, small groups, Bible studies, or other prayer groups.

Hopefully, in time, this can become more of a two-way partnership. But again, getting started is the key and sometimes getting started means doing a little less at first. And it is great when the teens request information on those who have adopted them!

3. Sunday School Exchange

A final concrete idea that some churches practice is something I call Sunday School Exchange (SSX). I realize some people claim that Sunday school is dead. Well, not in all contexts. However, if it is in yours, then figure out how to leverage this concept for your congregation (maybe it would be Small Group Exchange).

Some have noticed how often many of us are *all together separate* in our buildings on Sundays. Although all ages are represented, on a church campus most of the time those groups are segregated by age, even the various groups of adults. Young people are with other youth and older people are with mostly older folks. The age groups gather in classes or small groups, but these groups are typically homogeneous regarding generations. Instead of creating another program to connect folks, why not leverage those times to get the different generations together?

For this approach, a church can start as small as connecting two different classes or groups that are both on campus at the same time. The Sunday school hour can be a great time for some contexts to do this, but there is no reason the midweek time can't work as well. Obviously, first you must "sell" this concept to the different group leaders, but the vision of a time to simply connect generations is typically not a tough sale. In fact, I've found that the older generations are quick to embrace this opportunity; the young people might be more reticent. That's why there must be food involved!

Again, it may take time for this idea to germinate and for leaders to catch the vision. Be patient, keep asking folks to consider it, and educate them about the importance of "sticky relationships."[12]

The point of this gathering is to create an intentional time for younger and older folks to sit around tables together, share a light meal, and listen to each other talk. Some groups have a suggested guide for this time, and you will find some of these ideas in this book's Appendix.[13] Likely, in time, the groups will develop a feel for each other and be better at structuring their time than anyone else.

In one church, the fifth grade class was paired with the Old Testament class, which was led by a retired professor of the Old Testament. The guy was brilliant but not the most socially outgoing type. He was generally reserved but was totally gung-ho to connect with the fifth graders! He asked a person in his class to arrange the upcoming SSX. That leader got volunteers to bring lots of snacks, met with the fifth grade teacher, and made sure both groups were ready for their first meeting. The day of the meeting the adults brought tons of donuts and various juices.

The apprehensive fifth grade class made their way to the adult classroom at the appointed time. The OT class had space ready for them, and they did their best to keep a few kids together with a few of their own class members for small talk. After everyone had their snacks, the leader led a game and a slightly awkward time of discussion with ice-breaker questions. Not much "deeper" sharing occurred, but everyone seemed to have a decent time. Without too much pain, they made it through their first meeting and called it a moderate success.

The second time those two classes met for SSX the leader suggested that the OT class meet in the fifth grade classroom. The kids were ecstatic! That was their space and to have the adults coming there felt special—you could see it on their faces. The adults still brought food and drinks, but they truly wanted an "exchange" and so meeting in the others' space was important to them, as it was to the fifth graders.

Then the OT class teacher did the coolest thing—he challenged all the students to "sword drills." Know what that is? It's when a specific verse is given and the first person to find it in their Bible reads it aloud to everyone.

The kids did amazing . . . and barriers quickly evaporated as the OT teacher expertly provided verses that were funny, strange, and poignant. The group had such a good time! When the teacher was asked how the class went, his comment was, "It was the best class I've taught in thirty years." Wow! What a testimony of the importance and energy that comes from getting the young and old together and giving room to the Holy Spirit to work.

Doing something new will likely *not* be an immediate success. In fact, some may resist the change forever and argue that they "don't like it." With all love and respect in my heart, my response to that is, "So?" If we only did what we "like" then some of us might never get out of bed. The trajectory of these kinds of decisions is toward greater connection to and within the body of Christ. Getting there is vital. Precisely how we get there is open to discussion but currently, not much is facilitating this goal.

These kinds of connections begin to create a network of care around a young person that is much greater (and better!) than simply the youth minister frantically trying to keep up with each budding disciple in their charge. Better still? These connections are much more likely to last beyond the young people's time in the youth group because while youth workers are busily caring for the next generation of young people, the others in your faith community can continue their relationships with the Kevins and Jacks.

All this makes sense, right? It's also backed by research. The relationship a young person forms with a nonparental adult vitally contributes to that young person continuing in their faith journey into their twenties and beyond.[14] It just makes sense, and research attests that these relationships aid the process of lifelong faith.

These are simple ideas, and you'll probably come up with even better ones; when you do, please let me know! But I'm arguing that these should not be just fun, distracting things to do for the youth ministry but should become *central* to the practice of youth ministry in the body of Christ.

Parents/Guardians

According to the Think Orange organization, a typical church-attending young person spends forty hours with the youth group a year. Not much, eh? That same young person spends an average of three thousand hours with parents or guardians.[15] That one statistic seems to clarify where the most influence comes from in the young person's life. In fact, the National Study of Youth and Religion reports that "most U.S. teenagers mirror their parents' religious faith."[16]

Therefore, we cannot overemphasize the importance of meaningfully engaging with parents or guardians. (From here on out, I will use the designation "parents" to mean both parents and guardians.) And the implications for how we engage parents are a vital part of youth ministry. Strommen and Hardel report in *Passing on the Faith* that "close family relationships" are critical to faith formation and lifelong faith in young people.[17] They propose that family relationships can be strengthened through "parental harmony, effective communication, wise parental control and parental nurturing (of their children)."[18]

Now, let's be clear, some parents may never see you as "their" pastor, but to serve them in this capacity will require you to think pastorally in all your dealings with parents and families. And, to know what contributes to a family's relational strength can better equip you to act in ways that are congruent—rather than in opposition—to family strength.

One vital piece to doing this is to ensure clear and effective communication when it comes to the youth ministry. After all, parents cannot encourage their children to attend an event if they don't know about it (conversely, a teen may not receive permission to attend if they don't have information to provide to the parent). This will remove possible entry barriers to the programs, activities, and trips that are a part of the youth ministry. To ensure the barriers to entry are small or nonexistent, provide accurate, redundant, and way-ahead-of-time communication. It amazes me how this basic reality happens so infrequently in churches. Some seem to play hide-and-seek with dates, costs, or requirements of activities, or the information changes week to week. We must correct this to truly integrate youth and their parents into the body of Christ.

We must publish accurate information in a timely manner. I've learned that if we don't have next summer's youth mission trip or fall retreat on our calendar about twelve months ahead of time, some conflict will probably disable our kids from even having a chance to decide to go.

In his book *Sustainable Youth Ministry*, Mark DeVries argues for the critical nature of five "control documents"[19] of a *sustainable* ministry program. One of those is a twelve-month calendar. It is critical to plan. Even if a youth minister is in their first year of ministry at a church, that person will likely plan at least a few months in advance. After the first full twelve months of tenure, what has taken place over the past year is a good place to start for an annual calendar. Needless to say, this calendar will be deeply refined, changed, and edited over time, but it provides a basic template of what will happen in the future based upon what happened in the past. If it worked well to schedule the fall retreat two weeks before Thanksgiving, then do it again next year. (If it was a miserable failure, perhaps that is a good sign to rethink the timing . . . or potentially everything about it!)

A good way to contribute to advanced planning is to reserve a retreat facility at the end of the retreat—if you rebook, you may even get a discount for doing so twelve months out, or you may be able to at least roll your deposit over to the next reservation. In some contexts, if you don't book twelve months in advance, you won't find a facility simply because the demand is so high.

Once a facility is booked, the basic cost is already determined for the event and then the dates, location, and cost can be shared well in advance so some families can plan for the coming expense and the timing. A wonderful subsidiary benefit that can come for families, too, is that when dates are published in advance parents can plan their own "retreat," knowing the kids are occupied with trusted adults. If families don't know a major trip, event, or activity is coming with *lots* of notice, the youth may not be able to attend.

A few years back our family was planning an international trip to visit my wife's family in Ireland, Germany, and Switzerland. To get the best airline deals—and to coordinate our visit with family in three different countries—we had to plan months ahead. There had recently been a leadership transition in our youth ministry, and the youth mission trip dates were not yet chosen. Our kids both *loved* the youth group mission trip. However, as we saw the airline prices slowly start to creep up, we knew we had to secure our tickets. Based on the past timing of youth mission trips, we plotted our trip around our best guess of when it would be, booked airline tickets, and hoped for the best.

Sadly, the best didn't occur, and the youth mission trip dates finally were scheduled for right in the middle of our trip, causing much weeping and gnashing of teeth in our house. Our kids threatened not to go to Europe (they *really* looked forward to mission trips). It was a big deal for our family and caused stress and arguments in our home. The youth leadership team obviously intended no harm and were doing the best they could. Sadly, that didn't change the reality that our kids couldn't go simply because advance planning was not done. It's critical to remove all barriers for hyper-busy families by planning in advance.

Advance planning can also help to decrease or eliminate conflicts between grade-level programs within the same church. For families that have children spanning elementary, middle, and senior high school, wouldn't it be great if ministry leaders thought about how their plans affected families? For instance, perhaps if the high school group isn't meeting on a given night, then it may be a good idea if the middle school and elementary programs don't meet either. It's a way to keep from splitting families up on a given night and causing unneeded stress.

Conversely, if one program adds a weekly activity during the summer months, then the other should consider adding an activity to keep trips back and forth to church to a minimum. Clearly this isn't a case of "requirement" but for a church seeking to integrate young people, paying attention to the entire family system is required.

This accurate and advanced information needs not only to be published annually but also communicated repeatedly and in a timely manner—which means well ahead of payments being due. Perhaps four to six weeks in advance is a good rule of thumb—on the shorter end of that timeline for routine, lower-cost activities and on the longer end for weekend retreats or costly activities. And for multi-day or high-cost events, such as conferences, mission experiences, and camps, allow several months of advance notice.

Moreover, repeating this information is also a key element. Try to have a website or other resource that is *updated regularly* and will have all the basic information for parents and youth group members to check. What resource do you have that parents can rely upon to have the latest, greatest, and most up-to-date information? If you can't immediately answer that question, create that resource and begin to repeatedly communicate that it is *the* place to go when in doubt about an important detail. It doesn't need to be fancy; it just needs to be accurate and complete. This information site must cover all the basics: What. Where. When. How much. For whom. Purpose. Plan.

Another way to assist parents in nurturing young people beyond communication is to provide helpful resources for them as the primary caregivers in their kids' lives. One youth minister I know accomplishes this and repeated communication (two for one!) through a monthly electronic newsletter. This is a fantastic communication tool to provide highlights of what is coming each month. At the bottom of each newsletter, he also provides an article, tip, or current event in the lives of young people. He will hyperlink an article from the Fuller Youth Institute or other organizations about parents, social media, tech or phone use, etc.

These are great encouragements for parents and helpful reminders that they are not alone, that their youth pastor wants to help, and provides useful information to their email box twelve times a year. Some of the past articles have focused on having conversations with teens about faith, thoughts on mobile phone use for teens—when it is culturally appropriate to have a phone—information on current hot apps or video games, films or happenings in youth culture or the larger culture. Of course there are other resources like Commonsense Media, which I love because of its "commonsense" approach to navigating movies, films, books, apps, and video games.[20] Providing these kinds of resources is incredibly helpful for parents who need support and knowledge to help with the everyday decisions of being a parent.

Doug Fields argues that the most important part of recalibrating a ministry to be more attentive to the needs of the family "will be attitude rather than in direction or program components."[21] There is not a secret formula or specific programs that will make all the difference, but developing the critical nature to look at everything that is "youth ministry" in your context and bend it toward integration in the body of Christ or discarding it.

Intentionally Inviting Parents

Because youth group is the time for some teens to escape parental influence, when you plan to involve parents then they will need to be specifically invited. This opportunity to participate in youth group or a Bible study or even a retreat or trip can pay huge dividends in your move toward integration. Likely, the parents who participate will witness firsthand what an excellent, passionate, and thoughtful youth ministry you are leading. They'll enjoy their interaction with other teens and be delighted to see their own kids in a very different environment.

Now, if what you just read is fantasy for your context, I'd suggest you have some work to do before inviting parents into your program. But the sentiment is the same. Find safe and helpful places to invite parents and then do so on a regular basis. Some churches have an annual or biannual open house and parents are invited to attend the weekly youth ministry programs. These occasions highlight the good things happening in the ministry and involve parents as more than observers. They become participants who sing, pray, play, and converse just like everyone else. Since it's important to set these occasions up for success, personally invite some parents who will join in the fun and seriousness that you have planned.

I have found that inviting parents into what is happening can lead to larger invitations to participate not only in a weekly program but also in retreats, trips, and even short-term mission experiences. The fruit of those accepted invitations is difficult to accurately quantify. Often those parents became outstanding youth ministry advocates, connected with the youth on the trip (adding to the "sticky relationships" of those kids), and deepened their connection with their own child through a shared experience, not to mention the benefit to their own relationship with Christ. Study after study has shown a young person's well-being is most positively affected by the presence of parents who are engaged in their child's life.[22]

Parents as Youth Workers

Perhaps one of the most overlooked ways to integrate youth and adults more deeply into the body is through parents of teens volunteering with the youth group. In their pivotal work on the religious and spiritual lives of American teenagers reported in Soul Searching, sociologists Smith and Denton argue, "Youth ministry would probably best be pursued in a larger context of family ministry, that parents should be viewed as indispensable partners in the religious formation of youth."[23] Although this is not commonly practiced in many contexts and for too many years the popular model of youth ministry has "relied on pulling teens away from their parents," we have ended up with an enormous dropout rate of high school youth group grads simply because we've trained them that an integral relationship of their spiritual lives is the youth group rather than the body of Christ.[24] This single move is perhaps one of the most important because it has exponential effects on young people, the parent volunteers, and the congregation.

Have you ever seen a parent of one of your teens become a stark-raving-mad fan of something you are doing well in the youth ministry? By the grace of God, I have! That person spoke often and highly about our youth ministry to anyone and everyone who would listen, both inside and outside the church. That positive publicity came up in the most wonderful of places, such as church board meetings, with my lead pastor, and even among guests to our church. It was a gift that kept giving! Involving caring, committed, Christian parents is one of the best moves you can make to move toward the goal of integrating young people into the body of Christ.

Taking the Next Faithful Step

Finally, if we want to truly assist young people with integration into the body of Christ we need to provide consistent opportunities to deepen their spiritual lives. As Dr. Scott Cormode from the DuPree Center for Leadership often states, so much in leadership and life is about "taking the next faithful step."[25] Although the context from which Dr. Cormode is speaking is specifically about being a leader, the truth for our spiritual journey is obvious. How can we regularly, relentlessly, but without being a nag, provide opportunities for young people to take the next faithful step in their spiritual lives?

It's not enough to think of the youth group as monolithic (as previously discussed) but instead as a congregation of individuals who are each, likely, on different parts of this spiritual journey with various degrees of openness to go deeper. Some young people involved in the church simply want to "have fun" and hang out with friends in the youth group while others really want to know Jesus more intimately, and where else do you do that than at church?

So, while providing a safe, positive, and inviting place to "hang out" how do we also provide organic opportunities for our youth to put their toes in the water or advance on the adventure of following Jesus? That comes through intentional programming and a deep desire to see young people fall deeply, madly, and hopelessly in love with the Savior who loves them in the most rugged, scandalous, and irrational way they cannot imagine unless you assist them. We also presuppose that you are seriously on this journey yourself and leading your volunteers into deeper, more intimate communion with God and each other too! (More about that in the next section.)

Doug Fields was a master at just this thing . . . or perhaps it was his pastor Rick Warren from who he learned it. Nevertheless, in *Purpose-Driven Youth Ministry*[26] Fields spends six chapters making a case for the different spiritual commitments of people and how best to invite them into a deeper walk with Jesus. A key element in Fields's schema is that he has a programmatic pathway that intentionally addresses the various places of spiritual interest and depth. Because he has developed this so thoroughly and talks about it so regularly, the young people and adults involved in the ministry understand how best to, from a program stand-point, take the next faithful step.

Programs are not *the* answer, but they are a way to structurally address the various spiritual commitments in a group. It will take time. Fields mentioned that it took him five years at Saddleback to smooth this all out. If we don't program for the various spiritual depths, and don't provide structural opportunities to take the next faithful step, we are involving young people in the youth group but not in the body of Christ.

In this conversation about meeting young people where they are, it's important to state that for a youth worker from their church to not speak to youth, at some point, about their spiritual life is like visiting a doctor and never having them ask you about your health.

Imagine it, you set an appointment, you arrive on time, you pay your co-pay, and then you get shown to a room to wait for your fifteen minutes with your general practitioner. The doctor enters the room with a smile and begins to ask you questions about everything: How's work or school? How's the family? How's your team doing? Can you believe this weather? Done anything fun in the past month? Anything giving you joy lately, or grief? The questions continue until the fifteen minutes are up.

As you leave, you have a strange sense that the time you just spent there was "nice" and perhaps even "fun" but deeply frustrating since you never accomplished your purpose for making the appointment—to discuss the health issue you have been dealing with. Silly, isn't it? To consider seeing a doctor but not talking about your health. But when we develop relationships with young people in the context of the worshiping community and never seek spiritual conversations, never ask them how their prayer life is or if they ever read the Bible, it is just as silly and potentially frustrating for the young person.

Along this line of providing opportunities for young people to take the next faithful step is the posture with which we enter into relationship with each of them, regardless of their spiritual journey or openness. Conceivably, there is no better way to describe it than "holding the crown above their heads until they grow into it," as pastor Jerry Kester has said.

I believe that is a key part of youth ministry. Each person is a prince or princess by virtue of being a child of the King, and the entire process of our lives invites us to accept that truth, to believe it and allow it to form and inform our identity more than any of the other forces at work in our hearts and minds. Our job as youth worker (and parents) is to hold that crown of identity as a child of God, a child of the King, continually above the heads of the young people with whom we associate. We do this through words, actions, and most importantly, our example in how we validate and honor their humanity. We do harm to this vision when we dismiss their points of view or don't take their concerns seriously. In envisioning the good life with them, what do we show them? What are the values we express to those in our charge? That is the view we are pursuing of the good life and what we are implicitly communicating.

I hold the crown above their heads as I expect the best from young people but accept them when they do less. I hold the crown above their heads when I speak words of affirmation of their developing character and gently point out the places they may want to turn from—and stand with them regardless of how they choose. I hold the crown above their heads when I dream with them what life with Christ can be like beyond the youth group as they seek first the kingdom of God in high school, college, and by submitting their career choice to the wisdom and call of God. I hold the crown above their heads when I invite others who've overcome obstacles in their life to love God more fully with all of their life and show them examples of what fidelity to Jesus looks like at ages twenty, thirty, forty, fifty, seventy, and beyond. I hold the crown above their heads as I transparently (but appropriately) share my shortcomings, my temptations, and my failures with them because young people compare all they know about themselves with all they don't know about me. And lastly, I hold the crown above their heads when I allow the deep places in my heart to call out to the deep places in their hearts through place-sharing relationships of honesty and equality.[27]

We must make room for young people in the weekly rhythms of our congregational life by giving them places to serve, contribute, and speak. We must surround them with caring, committed Christian adults and make young people a priority everywhere, communicating clearly, redundantly, and way ahead of time with parents. We must create purposeful opportunities to go deeper by helping them take the next faithful step in their spiritual journeys. Unless and until we do these critical practices, we will not integrate young people into the body of Christ.

SECTION V
TOWARD A
TRANSFORMING
VISION OF MINISTRY FOR
SELF, OTHERS, AND
THE CHURCH

The Spirit of the Lord is upon me, because the Lord has anointed me. He has sent me to preach good news to the poor, to proclaim release to the prisoners and recovery of sight to the blind, to liberate the oppressed, and to proclaim the year of the Lord's favor.
—Jesus Christ
Luke 4:18–19, CEB

Adopt the same attitude as that of Christ Jesus,
who, existing in the form of God, did not consider equality with God as
something to be exploited. Instead he emptied himself by assuming the form of
a servant, taking on the likeness of humanity. And when he had come as a man,
he humbled himself by becoming obedient to the point of death—
even to death on a cross. For this reason God highly exalted him and gave him
the name that is above every name, so that at the name of Jesus every knee will
bow—in heaven and on earth and under the earth—and every tongue
will confess that Jesus Christ is Lord, to the glory of God the Father.
—Philippians 2:5–11, CSB

You can't lead what you won't live.
—Ed Stetzer[1]

All Christians are called to ministry, but some are called to *the* ministry.
—Keith Drury[2]

Ministry is the grateful response of God's people, whose activity in the world
and with one another suggests a new way of being alive. Ministry is not
something we "do" to someone else. It is a holy way of living toward
God and toward one another.
—*The Godbearing Life*[3]

The indictment to which contemporary youth ministry is vulnerable is
careless handling of the soul. We have related to youth admirably;
we play catch exceptionally well. But . . . we have failed to enlist them
in the missionary movement of Jesus Christ.
—*The Godbearing Life*[4]

SEVEN
It *All* Starts with You . . . Surprise!
• • • • • • • • • • • •

"MOST POLLS SAY that around seventy-five percent of Americans say they're Christians. Yet only about a quarter of Americans actually plan their lives around their religious faith."[1] Muse on that for a moment . . . three out of four Americans claim Christianity as the central philosophical organizing principle of their life (at least that is what it *should* mean to claim Christ), but only one out of four actually plan their lives around the teachings and person of Jesus Christ.

Do you have a problem with that? I certainly do. That sad reality is clearly reflected in the American church. In fact, research that has followed hundreds of young people over the course of several years demonstrates that the *de facto* belief system about God of churchgoing young people in America is what sociologist Christian Smith has labeled Moralistic Therapeutic Deism.[2] This belief system is based upon these five pillars of belief:

1. A God exists who created and orders the world and watches over human life on earth.

2. God wants people to be good, nice, and fair to each other, as taught in the Bible and by most world religions.

3. The central goal of life is to be happy and to feel good about oneself.

4. God does not need to be particularly involved in a person's life except when God is needed to resolve a problem.

5. Good people go to heaven when they die.[3]

As Princeton Practical Theologian and participating researcher on the National Study of Youth and Religion, Kenda Dean poignantly points out that the problem isn't with the young people who have articulated these beliefs as much as the problem is with the church (read: adults) who have inculcated those beliefs by their teaching and living example. Dean writes in *Almost Christian*:

The elephant in the room in the discussion about the National Study of Youth and Religion is the muddled ecclesiology of American churches, a confusion present, not only in young people but in congregations themselves. Put simply, *churches have lost track of Christianity's missional imagination*. We have forgotten that we are not here for ourselves, which has allowed self-focused spiritualities to put down roots in our soil. When practices intended to reflect God's self-giving love are cut off from their theological taproot in the *missio Dei*—God's sending of God's own self into the world in human form—these activities lose their ability to reflect outward, which weakens our resistance to spiritualities like Moralistic Therapeutic Deism. In the process, *we confuse Christianity with self-preservation*, which is the very opposite of Jesus's own witness, and the antithesis of his call to his disciples to take up their crosses and follow him. . . . The most likely explanation for Moralistic Therapeutic Deism is simply that *we reap what we sow*. We have received from teenagers exactly what we have asked them for: assent, not conviction; compliance, not faith. Young people invest in religion precisely what they think it is worth—and if they think the church is worthy of benign whatever-ism and no more, then *the indictment falls not on them, but on us*.[4]

Sorry if that stings a bit . . . well to be honest, I'm not sorry, but understand that this is written with tear-filled eyes, from a heart of love and with deep concern and commitment to the church and a passion for young and old to know and follow Jesus and experience the abundant life—the good life. And frankly, a report like this should sting. It should sting all of us. That is deeply troubling news about the church . . . about us—you and me. It calls us to examine not only our churches and ministries but also, perhaps more than anything else, our own lives.

What is the purpose of life? What is the goal—*telos*—of the good life? What do you believe it to be—because the young people and adults around you likely have an opinion from the way you live and act. How do you demonstrate your belief in that daily?

In *Leadership Starts with You,* Tim Milburn explains the importance of self-leadership before a person can lead anyone else. Tim quotes the Rhodium Rule, which states, "Do unto yourself what will inspire the best in others."[5]

We have to first lead ourselves in helpful ways toward wholeness and right priorities before we can inspire others to live out more fully what it means to carry out the mission of Christ in the world.

Please don't misunderstand me. I, in no way, mean to communicate that flawed, broken people cannot lead others—or none of us would be leading. I am arguing that we must understand our own brokenness and be in process toward health and wholeness as we encourage and lead youth and adults in those directions. That is the essence of self-leadership, being on the road, not necessarily at the destination.

Joe Gorman says it like this, "The well-being of the world starts with our own personal health."[6] It is essential that each of us, particularly those of us leading others, examine our unexamined assumptions about the point of life in all its aspects and submit them to the Holy Spirit's reanimation with a more Jesus-shaped vision. The words of the apostle Paul written to the church at Corinth come to mind, just as "God has reconciled us to himself through Christ and *gave us* the ministry of reconciliation . . . *we are therefore Christ's ambassadors,* as though God were making his appeal *through us*" (2 Corinthians 5:18, 20, emphasis added). This is a high calling. God is making his appeal through us . . . let's do our part to be good instruments.

This final section is perhaps more about the "vision of the good life" that our ministries and, more importantly, our lives reflect, which almost subliminally "teaches" others. What kind of values are implicit in the actions and interactions we have with others? For instance, do we "talk" of love, community, and each individual's importance and digni-ty—and then lead competitive games in such a way that demonstrates that our words are just "talk" because we actually harm the community and dignity and value of individuals with our not-so-good-natured trash-talk and win-at-any-cost attitude? Are we as leaders so concerned with pursuing victory that we bend the rules and, if we are honest, outright cheat simply because we are in charge so we can? Who is valued in our ministries (and lives)? Each person we encounter—or do we favor the athletic, talented, beautiful, or gifted?

Early in life, my sister taught me an important lesson about the val-ue of each person. I was in middle school and was fortunate to find my-self on the list of popular kids. I wasn't intentionally following Jesus but would have called myself a Christian. My sister gave me some advice. She simply said, "Mike, you're a BMOC (big man on campus), so be sure to be nice to the fat girls. I was a fat girl in junior and senior high, and the popular kids looked down on me. Don't be like them."

Although I'm not sure why, I had ears to hear that message from my sister, probably because I valued her opinion and she had invested in our relationship over the years despite the fourteen-year age gap be-tween us. I went to the school dance that year with a mission—to be nice to any "fat girl" I might encounter. I wasn't sure what that meant or how that resolve would be tested in next three hours. My friend Marty and I arrived at the dance fashionably late and hit the dance floor.

After several fast songs and nearly nonstop movement, a slow song came on. I was hot and sweaty and not really knowing what to do with a slow song anyway, so Marty and I decided to head to the bathroom—

an excellent hangout during school dances. Almost as soon as I turned around, I found Kerri standing in front of me looking expectant. My heart began beating rapidly. Kerri and I had a class or two together and were casual acquaintances. We were friendly but not good friends, and Kerri was significantly overweight.

"Hi, Mike," she said. "Do you want to dance?"

It was just the briefest of moments, but my seventh-grade mind raced through about ten thousand different ramifications of the choice before me. I saw my future both exploding with good and imploding with bad in the blink of an eye, all based on how I would answer. Then I recalled my conversation with my sister. I imagined the pain my sister had suffered through her teen years and decided I wasn't willing to inflict any pain like that in someone else's life. So I smiled and said yes.

We awkwardly danced through that three-minute song by Journey and then parted ways. I finally got to the bathroom, where Marty was wondering what had happened to me. I felt a strange warmth in my heart for doing something that mattered. I decided I kind of liked that feeling. Kerri asked me to dance several more times throughout our middle and high school years, and I never said no. In fact, I even developed the maturity to ask her a time or two in those years.

Saying yes to Kerri was not an earthshaking decision, yet it was for an ego-fragile, seventh-grade boy. Many years later I found out it was significant to Kerri too. Kerri died a few years ago. Before a disease slowly stole her life, she reached out to me. She had been reflecting on her life and wanted to let me know how our dances together throughout middle and high school provided much joy and affirmation and created a sense of acceptance for her.

I couldn't have been more grateful for her thoughtfulness to let me know. The fact that those small decisions had a larger impact for Kerri than I realized at the time made my heart swell with gratitude. That first yes set me on a trajectory that shaped my behavior not only at dances but also in my daily life. I realized there were not popular kids and unpopular kids. There weren't cool kids and uncool kids. There weren't some kids who had more value than others—there were just kids.

And we all fit that category. All of this was thanks to my sister, who cared enough to share one little piece of advice with her punky brother one night. And it's imperative advice for our youth ministries.

When teenagers walk into our church—and perhaps especially into our youth space—it should be unlike any other environment they enter. They must encounter affirmation, acceptance, love, and complete safety—both physical and emotional. It cannot be a place where a kid is fearful or may be excluded for any reason. It must be a place where adults *and* kids learn to live and love like Jesus.

It won't be perfect; there will be failure along the way, but the trajectory of the ethos of your group *must* be affirmation, acceptance, and love for all. How does that start? By your modeling affirmation, acceptance, and love for all. Your expectation that other youth workers do the same and in your explicit teaching young people that this is what our group is about.[7] Some will push back, but you *will* win in time, if you are persistent and hang around long enough to see it.

James K. A. Smith writes persuasively about the power of choice in his fascinating book *You Are What You Love*. He argues that humans are indelibly shaped into whatever they most crave or want. He argues that those longings are essentially "love" expressed, even though we may never admit those longings are things we rationally "love." However, Smith reasons, one's "deepest desire is the one manifested by your daily life and habits."[8] In example, we may say we deeply value (have longings for, desire and even "love") to be healthy, but if our daily practice is to overeat fast food, not exercise, sleep little, and live on caffeine, then clearly our actual love is not for health, but for whatever else we choose.

The good news? Humans can *choose* to change longings, cravings, and deep desires in order to "love" correctly.

Toward the end of my college experience and my formal participation in organized sports, I was without a routine workout schedule.

For the previous eight-plus years, getting exercise was simply a part of my daily schedule. From the time I was twelve until my early twenties I found a regular schedule of exercise in organized, competitive sports. After my last season as a thrower in college, I found myself without this routine. I was a relatively poor college student and a bit undisciplined in my eating, and I was gaining weight and size.

I realized something needed to be done. My roommate was a runner. He was fit and seemed to enjoy going out for runs several times each week. I thought this was my answer. I would run. The only problem was that I hated running. However, I could afford a pair of inexpensive running shoes but not a monthly gym membership, so I decided that I would run. I purchased the shoes, sought advice from my roommate, and set off on my first run. Although it was more of a short jog-walk-panting-near-death experience, I did it. The next day I was sore in places I didn't know I had muscles. I walked strangely, and I had a blister on my pinky toe. I didn't love it, but I had decided to run, and I did. That made me proud.

Within six weeks, running had become a habit. I now knew several routes I could run depending upon how I felt and the time I had. My toe developed a callous and hadn't hurt for weeks. Additionally, I had lost several pounds and my pants fit much more like they had in the past. Astonishingly, I felt really good after my runs and had increased my pace and distance. In fact, if I didn't run for two days in a row, I missed it!

Running had become my habit, my friend, and a source of not only physical health but also mental health. When I had a bad day, I could run and feel better. My *decision* to run had developed a *desire* to run and even a *love* for running—but that all started with a rationale choice.

We choose how we live, relate to others, and model the journey with Christ each day. We do not have to be captive to how we "feel" or what we have done in the past.

The practice of youth ministry is no different, and simply because a particular way of "doing" youth ministry has been modeled does not mean it is the right way. It is worth reflection and examination of the outcomes. Further, whatever is *actually* taking place in the context of your ministry with young people is by your choice. So, what are you choosing?

I am confident by now that it is abundantly clear that this final part of this project is more about your own heart and life practice than the outward shape of your ministry program . . . primarily because I believe the former will significantly shape the latter. For far too long our youth ministries have been places that simply reflect the values, attitudes, and vision of the good life of our secular culture. This final section is attempting to get at the pervasive and elusive ethos of a youth ministry, and to point out the importance that that ethos must be one of affirmation, acceptance, love, accountability, discipline, and, in short, that it's thoroughly Christian. I'm writing about this at the end because I want it to stick. Perhaps all the other stuff is much more easy to assimilate and enact. This, however, is really the heart of the matter and the key to all else if young people will ever truly be introduced into the mission of Christ.

Kenda Dean's stinging indictment of the American church and how we are complicit in the formation of moralistic therapeutic deists is not left like a dangling modifier; she shares four "cultural tools" of the "highly devoted" teenagers—which represent about eight percent of American youth—that came through in her involvement with the NSYR study. The study defined "high devoted" teens as those who:

- attend religious services weekly or more
- place very or extremely high importance on faith in their everyday lives
- feel very or extremely close to God
- are involved in a religious youth group
- pray a few times a week or more
- read Scripture once or twice a week or more[9]

The cultural "tools" that contribute to the formation of highly devoted young people are:

- They confess their tradition's creed or God-story.

- They belong to a community that enacts the God-story.
- They feel called by this story to contribute to a larger purpose.
- They have a hope for the future promised by this story.[10]

It's important to understand that the presence of these tools does not guarantee a lifelong faith, but to understand that these are a part of the picture of those young people who seem to be on a trajectory to most likely continue this path. How can we emphasize these cultural tools in our own ministries?

They Confess Their Tradition's Creed or God-story

For many years now, before entering the youth group, young people in our church go through a ten-week catechism class that leads to Easter, and opportunities to become a member of the church and receive the sacrament of baptism. This systematic, annual curriculum seeks to ensure that young people are exposed to the Wesleyan tradition and its doctrine and nuanced views of humanity, sin, redemption, salvation, entire sanctification (growth in grace), and eternity. They also meet and connect with many different adult mentors and pastors in our church. They are able to ask about the sanctuary, its furniture, the structure of our worship, and the "why?" behind the way things are. They also have an opportunity to practice some of the classic spiritual disciplines of the church.

Those young people who feel a sense of connectedness and kinship with these beliefs have opportunity to take the next faithful step of membership and/or baptism. Now clearly, youth in sixth grade are just beginning to experience the early stages of abstract thought. Doctrine and theology can be just that—a bit abstract. How much can they really absorb and understand? That is very individualistic. However, this early exposure, and the follow-up that happens in the youth ministry, gives youth an opportunity to hear, clearly and in detail, just what Wesleyans believe about life and its purpose. This is a valuable and important act for the church to provide and, frankly, to repeat often! But these details help to bring into focus what takes place in the context of the weekly worship services and why the pastor explains some things differently than the church down the street. This is extremely important if these youth will ever make these beliefs their own.

By providing a systematic opportunity for young people to grasp and understand a community's distinct God-story, we honor young people with the invitation to enter into that story.

They Belong to a Community That Enacts the God-story

For a community to enact the God-story, a congregation must be immersed in and rehearse their God-story routinely. The Christian calendar and lectionary offer an excellent structural approach for a community to be systematically exposed to the entirety of the God-story. As we walk through the *seasons* of the Christian year along with the accompanying biblical texts provided, over a three-year cycle, the congregation will be exposed to all major biblical stories and passages. When a worship team or other leader decides on teaching, they have a tendency, over time, to return time and again to the team or leader's pet themes. Over time, this can lead to a lack of acquaintance with the corpus of Scripture. By using the lectionary, a leader deals with various narratives in Scripture they may never have chosen to teach or preach on. After all, who wants to exegete the story of Tamar and Judah or the rape of Dinah, or the entire books of Numbers or Leviticus? But when we avoid difficult passages and subjects, we are not feeding God's flock a holistic diet. In avoiding the difficult stories and subject matter, we may unwittingly withhold the very key that unlocks a people' slavery.

The Christian calendar also provides a needed rhythm to the life of worship that shapes a community in important ways. There are times of waiting and anticipation (Advent); somber reflection and lament (Lent and Holy Week); grand, ecstatic celebration (Easter); and the daily call of faithfulness during most of the cycle, appropriately entitled ordinary time. The Christian year and the lectionary invite us to find our own experiences aligned with the experiences of those sisters and brothers of the past who have struggled to walk faithfully before God. Learning about their lives, struggles, failures, and missteps helps not only to unite our lives across the millennia but also to see that what we experience is part of the human condition. That is a source of comfort and even grace for those of us who can feel at times like lonely pilgrims on this journey. Our spiritual ancestors struggled in ways that are similar to ours—although in very different contexts, for sure—but with similar situations with family, superiors, money, lust, power, greed, and more. These tools are not fail-safe, but they allow the Spirit room to meet the needs of our community by our trust in the silent rhythms of God's grace working through them.

They Feel Called by This Story to Contribute to a Larger Purpose

This is about developing a sense of vocation for one's life. This is great truth not only for young people but for each of us, for in this "tool" is a recognition that the gospel and the life, death, and resurrection of Jesus Christ call me not just to a decision to pray a prayer of repentance, but to a decision to submit my choices, my daily living, my career choice, and indeed, my entire existence to my Lord . . . or at least to be on that trajectory (there's that word again!). The apostle Paul reinforced this message in 1 Thessalonians 5:23-34 when he wrote:

> May God himself, the God of peace, sanctify you through and through. May your whole spirit, soul and body be kept blameless at the coming of our Lord Jesus Christ. The one who calls you is faithful, and he will do it.[11]

Our "whole" selves are the focus of God's redemption and sanctification. Every aspect of our personhood is to be preserved for God and to be used in service to God. For far too long, we have focused only upon heaven in the future instead of the kingdom that has come, here and now. And so, this must affect our daily lives, and this must be modeled and communicated to young people systemically . . . through our lives. This recognition has led to creation care movements within the church—where all aspects of the created order are respected and nurtured. It has implications for how we spend our time, money, the products we purchase, the way we do business and with whom, the food we serve, the activities we plan, and so on. Our faith lives are not disconnected from our school lives, work lives, and family lives.

By emphasizing this reality to young people, we can help them to see the ways their choices every day can be ways to practice their faith. To be whole (mature) is to be an integrated self. How do we teach this to young people? How we live is the most important aspect of this, and it is part of the reason I sought to make compassionate service the centerpiece of the youth ministry calendar I constructed.

Now to bring this down from such an abstract level let me suggest this: Look over your youth ministry calendar. What is emphasized week to week, in a month, and over the course of a year? What are the "traditions" and expectations of younger kids as they move into the youth group? Are they comprised of dreams like, "I can't wait to be in the youth group because they do a trip to Disneyland every year!" Or "I love the youth group because our youth pastor really gets us!" Or "I love this youth group because we really love each other and are learning together how best to love the world every day."

Now, those might not be *their* words, precisely, but what do they see and expect? Another way to think about it is discerning the youth ministry's "centerpiece." Is it a trip, retreat, or an annual or quadrennial conference? Is it a mission experience or compassionate service?

What is the organizing principle of your youth ministry—to keep kids engaged in church activities and, thus, out of trouble? Or is it to change them and their world by introducing them to life-giving service over just Christian entertainment. How is the ministry constructed to invite young people into a purpose—and to develop a sense of vocation—that is larger than themselves? How does it model and enflesh, "preach good news to the poor, . . . proclaim release to the prisoners and recovery of sight to the blind, . . . liberate the oppressed, and . . . proclaim the year of the Lord's favor" (Luke 4:18–19, CEB)?

Now, let me be clear, I do not think this is an either-or situation. I do not advocate for all work and no play. I'm all about having a good time, laughter, and fun . . . just sit in on one of my classes and see how, in one hour, I laugh and cry almost every day!

What I'm trying to get at is this: What is the purpose for life being modeled throughout the year in your youth ministry? To have fun? Eat lots of pizza, watch movies, and play cool games? Or maybe sing lots of worship songs and feel really "spiritual"? Or maybe go to camp each summer, cry at the end of the week, and make commitments that no one asks about until the next summer? Or could it be possibly about learning to give your life away in order to find it—and having this modeled through the adult leaders in the group and even some of the activities the youth group participates in?

I learned from a youth ministry *master*. I volunteered with him and then became his associate over the course of four-plus years. The centerpiece of his entire twelve-month calendar? Service. Whether it was serving Communion or taking an offering, doing chores and maintenance around the church building, volunteering at the local rescue mission, doing yard work for the elderly, widowed, and shut-ins from our church, or the annual youth mission trip, service was what this youth ministry was about. He was so focused on getting young people to learn the magic of giving away their lives that, one year, the youth group took on the literacy program for all of Shelter KC (formerly Kansas City Rescue Mission). Yep, teens teaching adults how to read every week. It was amazing!

Again, don't be mistaken, a lot of fun happened along the way. There were retreats, Nerf wars, crazy scavenger hunts, large outreach events, days at the beach, and more, but the foundation of all that was done every year was service. The apex was the annual mission trip. The youth pastor believed that a mission experience was not about tourism or a chance to travel somewhere to visit an amusement park or other attraction but a disciplined opportunity to challenge oneself and, on purpose, deny oneself through kenotic work for several days, while living in humble community—all in hopes of improving the world through the sacrificial work completed by a group of unskilled high school laborers. The mission trip typically lasted ten days, but preparation began in December for a June trip. So this experience was actually a six-month journey.

Those in the community made frequent reference to the upcoming trip or past trips. It was looked forward to with expectation as an on-purpose decision to submit ourselves to living the Christ life for ten days and seeing what came from it. The mission trip offered young people an experiment of sorts to walk away from all that was familiar and comfortable—no phones or technology. Instead, they disconnected so they could reconnect with God and others. It was an experience that never disappointed. It created a window for all participants to see another way of living, and some of us were forever changed by that vision. In fact, I found in more than a decade of leading these kinds of "strict, no-fun" trips, kids only asked to do them more instead of complaining about the dumb rules that involved no personal technology or even music for the twenty-two-hour-one-way drive.

On such a trip, I experienced the most amazing encounter with the "resurrection life" of Jesus among us. It was a hot day, just like they all were. We had actually completed the house we had arrived to build the previous day. Our kids had worked hard, effectively, and efficiently. We were all tired, but we had come to work the entire week, and that was what we would do. In fact, when we completed our house, some teens were concerned there was nothing more to do. As I talked with our supervisor about the next day's activities, he shared some of the options for our group. First, he suggested we simply have a tourist day and visit the town square and do a little shopping, eat some local food, and go to the beach.

I knew our group would enjoy that, but that was not what they had come to do. He then described some of the unfinished projects. There were houses that needed to be roofed, others that needed stucco, and still more that needed walls built. Then he paused and said there was one particular project that was really tough due to its location. It was a piece of land that the family had saved for many months to purchase, and they were so proud they now owned it. However, it was located behind another completed house and had no easy access for people, let alone building supplies.

I asked what stage it was in, and he said it hadn't even been started. That meant the ground needed to be leveled, and then nearly eight tons of concrete would have to be mixed by hand, poured, screeded, and troweled. It sounded like an ambitious project for a group that was already tired from seven days of travel and work, but I decided to leave the decision to the group.

That night, during our time of debriefing, the supervisor joined us. He again laid out the various choices the group had for the coming day. Although everyone dreamed of putting their toes in the sand at the beach, when he explained about the difficult site and how, if we could get the foundation laid, it would be a huge encouragement to both the family and the next group that came to build, the group deliberated only a few moments. They decided we'd get up bright and early and do the concrete. I couldn't have been prouder of this group. They came to serve, and they were doing that until the very end!

The next day when we arrived at the site, it was worse than we imagined. The place was a challenge to get to, and we had no idea how we'd get our tools and building supplies in. Not only that, but the site was small, so our group of twenty-eight couldn't even work on it together. It had been dug out of the hillside, and the space provided barely enough room for the eleven-foot by twenty-two-foot foundation and a small space to walk around once the house was completed.

I wondered if we had chosen badly. After some time, we discovered that, above the building site, on what just appeared to be a hill, was a primitive road we could access with our truck. After more investigation we found the road that led to a place just above the building site and determined we could safely deliver the building supplies from there. It would be much easier to drop the supplies down to the site rather than carrying them around the small easement of the completed house.

Once we started to see how our workflow might progress, we split into groups with the assigned tasks of loading supplies, transporting supplies, carefully dumping supplies down the side of the hill, and then mixing the concrete onsite. After just sixty to ninety minutes, we were working! The team was broken up into several smaller teams, and we hummed along like a fine sewing machine. Each part was doing what it needed, when it was needed, and we were in a serious groove. It was amazing!

The excitement and rhythm of our work were palpable. The supervisor stopped by shortly after we got started and expressed his amazement not only at our organization but also the energy and enthusiasm of everyone working hard and in sync! As he stood by, I noticed he started his stopwatch. After we finished, he said he could tell by the way we were working that we presented a serious threat to the organization's record time for mixing and pouring a single house foundation. It was as if the Spirit were orchestrating each aspect of the work on the site and in each of us . . . orchestrating and persuading us individually and collectively to work as one body. Words do not adequately describe what we experienced that day. Even now, I feel a pulse of that excitement I felt as I looked at our group and noticed how quickly the mixed concrete was filling the forms we had built just an hour before. We were experiencing the resurrection life of the body of Christ. Never before had I experienced that so powerfully.

The next day we packed up and drove part of the way home. We didn't go to Disneyland or other amusement parks because that wasn't the point. Instead, we went to a hotel and spent a day decompressing, relaxing, being together, getting clean, and starting the process of synthesizing what had just taken place in each of us and in our group. Although it wasn't a lot of time, it was enough to think about how we would go back to places to live with others who didn't know what we now did, who hadn't experienced what we had experienced, and to consider how to live with them in a way that contributed to harmony and peace.

What these trips have demonstrated to me time and again is the power of working toward a goal as a group with a single-minded focus on a worthy project for others. And I've also learned it's not enough to simply go and participate in this project each summer. But coming home from this trip begs us to ask, "So how will we live now?" This question crept into our souls in a way I had not experienced before and into the souls of some of my teens, and they began, slowly, to live differently because of it.

Erin came home and asked her parents to decide the amount of money that would be used for her annual fall school shopping trip. She then received permission to take that money, use a small portion to purchase clothes from a thrift store (thrift storing wasn't cool then), and send the remaining money to the family whose house we built.

Stephanie came home and decided to volunteer in the local nursing home. I didn't know about this until weeks later, when we were trying to find a time to meet for coffee and she wasn't available on Tuesday afternoons because she volunteered at the nursing home on Tuesdays after school. When pressed, she reluctantly shared about giving the female residents pedicures. She began by washing and rubbing their feet and finished by applying a fresh coat of paint to their toes. This blew me away.

"How did you get started doing this?" I asked. "Do you have a parent or relative who works there, who lives there?"

"No," she commented. "I just wanted to keep the things I encountered on the mission trip alive in my life back home."

Kendra came home with new eyes to see the great needs around her. She saw loneliness in her peers' lives in the high school—loneliness that had always been there that she had never taken time to notice. She began eating lunch with people who didn't seem to have any friends. One came to church with her and came to know Jesus in a personal way.

The stories could go on and on, but the coolest thing was that none of the kids did something that was suggested or encouraged. They simply caught the vision of living less myopically than they had, and chose to see others around them. They came to see part of what it means to live the mission of Jesus; to purposefully look for others who need care and actively care for them.

They continued to be normal kids, of course. But they also continued to be people who were changed because they encountered the Christ life among our group in the dirt of a Mexico mission trip.

The mission trip isn't the point—it was simply a vehicle for experiential learning about the abundant life of Christ that comes to us as we serve, give, and share. These trips are a way to find the wholeness of life during a short, experimental time period by living more closely to the way that Christ lived, which enables us to imagine living differently—in large and small ways—every day. Mission trips give us a larger perspective view of our lives. They help us to get out of our tiny worlds by disconnecting us from distractions and connecting us to relationships with peers, the needs of others, and our own selves—often through uncomfortable circumstances.

Yes, I believe in the mission trip experience. Not mission-tourism, not going to exotic places to shop or to a neighborhood near Disneyland so we can endure some service projects to feel good about paying $120 each to ride the Matterhorn, but rather for the long van ride of conversations, sleeping, and no radio.

A mission experience is, at best, only a limited glimpse of the kingdom life . . . and yet a critical one. The real test comes in the opportunities provided to continue to serve following the trip and throughout the year. The youth ministry is structured best when service, ministry, generosity, and hospitality are woven throughout the entire twelve-month cycle and not on an isolated trip. However, the trip can be a most excellent experiment for youth to see the life-giving nature of something like pulling weeds at the home of an elderly resident in the community. It can also help them to see that their whole life presents invitations to be bent toward service and setting the world to rights.

One youth pastor friend figured this out and, over time, led a growing number of young people in biweekly service projects during youth group. The craziest part? The kids loved it! Service, of this kind, becomes an act of subversion of the importance I can feel to have things "my way" and to fulfill "my desires" over the needs of others. It helps to model for others how to live *Christianly*. Don't misunderstand, however. Kids loved it because they were led, over the course of *years* to slowly, incrementally see the value of service. That is a truly a holy way of living among others. This is about developing a vision for life that is about a larger purpose.

They Have a Hope for the Future Promised by This Story

To do this well, the young people need to have transparent adult friends to journey with them. These adults can embody what this hope looks like. They can also ask good questions and be sounding boards for the dreams of young people. In their best form, these relationships will be ones in which each party can learn from the other in transparent and vulnerable ways (place-sharing). They may also be natural places where both members take the next faithful step in their own journeys, even if those two journeys are in very different places.

Let me illustrate. I started saving for retirement when I was about twenty years old. An economics professor turned me onto the concept of becoming a millionaire—not by striking it rich but through disciplined saving over my entire working lifetime. I bought in hook, line, and sinker. Essentially, he argued if a person set aside 10 percent of all they ever earned in an interest-bearing investment (preferably a mutual fund) then, given the historic return of the stock market (about 10 percent then), they should accumulate about $1 million by the time they reach retirement age.

Being a person of faith, I decided that I would first tithe 10 percent. Besides being an act of faithfulness to God, tithing is an act of rebellion against the prevailing greed, selfishness, and tyranny of accumulation for myself. It's an act of expression of the abundance of God's resources against the sense of scarcity that can be so much a part of our world. After tithe, I decided to invest 10 percent (today this plan requires more like 14 to 15 percent) and live off the rest.

As I grew in my journey with Jesus I struggled, at times, with monthly setting aside a substantial portion of money for this goal of being "rich" in my later years. I struggled to find a right heart about that sum of money—particularly as it grew larger than my annual salary. I sensed a weakness in myself to become obsessed with the sum even to the point of worship. I struggled because the narrative of our culture shaped my perspective on retirement and the good life. I was uncomfortable with that but didn't have a better view at the time. In my better moments I thought of it as stewardship and doing everything in my power to be a good steward with the resources God had provided for my family and me. I think that is true. At the same time, however, retirement, in my mind, was often associated with a life of leisure, doing whatever pleased me, and generally, a selfish, self-focused, and self-consumed existence.

Sadly, that was my vision of the retirement good life. It hadn't occurred to me how disjointed that view was from my view of the good life of preretirement that included community, service, and worship. Over time my discomfort came to be closely associated with my 403(b) and, frankly, I didn't know how to reconcile that. It was a strange sort of dance of discomfort yet gratitude, since this discipline was "paying off" with a sum that was substantial after nearly thirty years of disciplined saving and compound interest.

Then a friend seriously challenged my theology of retirement. He called out my view of the good life with a right reading of Genesis (and all of Scripture) and told me that to be human is to be productive and

148

to contribute. He exclaimed that he didn't see anyone "retire" (meaning to cease being productive or cease contributing) in the Old or New Testaments. He pointed out that the notion was invented by our modern, affluent society and was incompatible with the kingdom view of the purpose of human life. He then reframed what a funded retirement could look like that was much more generative. He talked about the resource it could provide for two things: generosity to others, and productivity in the church and world without the need to be paid.

At first, I wasn't convinced. Prima facie, "generosity" and "working but not being paid" weren't appealing prospects, but God began to reshape my heart. In time, the Spirit began to play with my imagination, and those two concepts became extremely animating prospects to me. I began to dream of burdensome debt we could redeem for needy people, the way we could bless individuals, families, or even small churches . . . for Sandy and me to be able to serve areas that may not have access to or the resources to afford the services we could give.

Those were stimulating dreams! And they began to generate, deep in my soul, a burning passion to be in a financial position to live them out. Today our motivation for saving is multifaceted: stewardship (being as responsible as we can with the resources God richly provides), generosity toward others, and serving and producing without the need for compensation. I'm not sure if this is the final place where I'll land, but it seems much closer to alignment with the life and purpose of Jesus Christ than living a life of leisure.

How does this relate to a hope for the future? My vision for retirement was the same narrative of the prevailing culture in which I lived. The good life is about people accumulating enough to spend their final days in relative luxury, doing only what they want without responsibility or requirement.

That story did not provide a generative hope for my future. However, my community (embodied by my running partner) shared a different story that was counter to the dominant narrative of retirement. This engendered a great hope for my wife and me as to the purpose of our lives when we reach a time when we won't need to work for compensation. That is the gift of the Christian community, and this kind of counter-cultural hope is precisely what young (and not so young) people need to move to the third quarter of life successfully and Christianly.

Bottom line: The decisions you make, the way you spend your money and time, and the entire direction of your life . . . is it Christ-focused? I'm talking about the general trajectory of your entire life . . . because you do what you love! And this is revealed in the structure, form, and calendar of your youth ministry.

I have recently conducted qualitative research regarding faith-based internships with participants from five different ministry organizations (only one was a church). I learned some extraordinary things—such as how many of these interns picked up practices and even changed the direction of their lives as a result of their internship. They served for a year or more with committed, caring, Christian people, and that influence and environment literally shaped their lives for years into the future. Some former interns had completed their internships nearly twenty years before my interview. The daily interactions you have with young adults and adolescents might be a moment they look back on and say, "That was when everything changed for me." What we are doing matters, and it matters a great deal.

I am not precisely sure how best to get at this idea of integrating young people into the mission of Jesus Christ. What I know, however, is that if we don't make intentional, repeated, and concentrated effort to do this in a variety of contextually appropriate ways, if we don't bend our messages and the very thrust of our ministry with youth toward this end, young people may never get an opportunity to really come to know the freedom of the sanctified life and the experience of having a purpose for living that is so much larger and more important than the American Dream. We must elevate the practice of youth ministry from the previous generationally insulated, entertainment-based programming that focused on making kids happy and catering to their desires instead of providing systemic connections to caring, committed, Christian adults. Connections anchor youth to the body of Christ. We must seek to provide glimpses of the kingdom and the beauty of faithful living, which is a part of the abundant life we are all hoping to live—even though we often seek it in unfulfilling ways marketed to us by the commercial economy that saturates us with images of the good life that, ultimately, leave us isolated, lonely, and in debt.

So, examine your heart and life, endeavor to live Christianly, invite others to do that with you, and then seek to minister to the youth in your community in ways that invite them to do the same.

Perhaps what I really believe is closer to this definition of the *telos* of youth ministry: *The purpose of youth ministry is to integrate young people into the body of Christ and provide accurate glimpses of the kingdom of God so that they may experience an invitation to join the mission of Christ.*

Truth be told, I'm uneasy with the idea of literally integrating youth into the mission of Christ. There are so many reasons why that simply is too lofty a goal for work with twelve- to eighteen-year-olds. Most of them just aren't at a place to truly make that commitment in high school, and I don't want to contribute to their identity foreclosure. However, I do believe we can provide glimpses of the kingdom and the good life that will never be erased from their memory. Those memories can be employed by the Holy Spirit in their imaginations and offered as invitations to join the Spirit in what the Spirit is doing in the world. And to do that is truly to invite young people to be integrated into the body of Christ and into the mission of Christ.

EIGHT

The *Imago Dei* and Missional Ministry to Youth

by Tom Combes

● ● ● ● ● ● ● ● ● ● ● ●

Introduction

When I was a youth ministry volunteer, I often met with several other youth workers for breakfast at a restaurant located between several schools, where students often stopped in before school. One day an eleventh grader who was involved in our youth group came in to eat with us and she told me that she was anxious about a particularly stressful situation she would face later that day at school. Wanting to reassure her, I said, "Just be yourself."

I obviously struck a nerve because she shot back at me, "But I don't know *who that is!*"

This high school student's response was a poignant reminder of a fundamental developmental task for all adolescents: answering the question "Who am I?"

Adolescents constantly respond one way or another to their internal drive to settle this question of identity. Developmentally speaking, as young people exit childhood and enter into adolescence, a new consciousness begins to emerge; that of becoming a "self" with its own unique "being," the way they see themselves and define themselves as "me."[1] This awareness of their future existence as an adult brings an upheaval of the ways they related to their world when it was the relatively small space of childhood. They are moving into a new realm where the space is now essentially the *entire universe*. This results in a keen perception that they are, on the one hand, restless to discover that new, unique self while, on the other hand, existing on the verge of "nothingness," of being swallowed up in the cosmos.[2] Adolescents live with the deep awareness that everything seems like life or death, from one extreme to another, that their very being walks a thin line between possibility and nothingness, with an underlying angst that they really don't know who they are.[3]

The essence of God's work in the world—and therefore the essence of missional ministry—is that there is a means to "life the way it was meant to be." This is *the* grand narrative, the long arc of God, as Father, Son, and Holy Spirit at work in the world to come to his people, to purify them and make them his own possession. This is what theologians call the *missio Dei.*[4] The result of this mission is what Hebrew speakers of the Bible knew as *shalom,* meaning flourishing, peace, wholeness, and delight.[5] *Shalom* is the life-giving answer to "Who am I?" because it is precisely and fully the life all humans were created for. It is at the heart of the good news of the gospel. Missional ministry to youth, then, is cooperating with this *missio Dei,* through the power of the Holy Spirit, to bring *shalom* to bear, through the death and resurrection of Jesus, in the lives of teenagers, by entering their world *incarnationally* to form unconditional friendships and proclaim this gospel.

The task of missional ministry begins by interpreting the world of adolescents through the lens of the *missio Dei,* and then creating ministry actions that bring *shalom* to bear in their lives, trusting that these Spirit-cooperating actions (praxis) will share in the forming of the new "me." Adolescents ask, "Who am I?" This hope of the gospel for adolescents is that it leads them into *the* narrative that ultimately offers them salvation *from* the devastating effects of sin and offers them salvation *to* shalom and wholeness.

Looking Through the Lens of the *Missio Dei*

What, then, should evangelism to youth look like when their driving quest is to answer the question "Who am I?" in a world where the institutions, such as church, family, civic involvement, and education that used to help us understand ourselves and our beliefs are eroding to the point of irrelevancy, where our technology is promising us life and draining us at the same time, and where the general opinion about religion is rooted in moralistic, therapeutic deism? In this reality, there is no pathway to *shalom,* no answer to "Who am I?" Missional ministry to youth needs to aim for both at the same time.

The *missio Dei* has always been about restoring *shalom* and, as a result, bringing true identity to God's redeemed people.[6] Today this grand story of restoration and redemption is eclipsed by the smaller stories most teenagers have accepted as normal (as well as shrunken) versions of life. However, the moon eclipses the sun not because it is bigger or more powerful, but because it blocks the view.

The eclipse is something of a metaphor for the effects of sin. Today teenagers are given over to the drama of this dehumanizing and despairing world not because it is more powerful than God's mission but because it's in the way. Evangelism, then, is *reversing the eclipse*—painting the picture of God's work, through Jesus, to exchange the small, dehumanizing story of the world around them for God's larger, life-giving, *shalom*-bearing story of life the way it was meant to be.

If missional ministry to youth is about reversing the eclipse so that the true story comes to light, it must be firmly rooted in the larger story of the *missio Dei.* This story begins where God began his story of identity—human beings created in his image—and it ends where we were designed to be all along: "fully renewed, image-bearing human beings."[7] Ministry never gets enough theological and developmental traction if it only describes the "end" (e.g., being a "new creation" [2 Corinthians 5:17]; having life "to the full" [John 10:10]) without also considering God's missional trajectory, including its beginning point in creation.[8] It is one thing to affirm, in an abstract or matter of fact sense, that humans are created in God's image (Genesis 1:26–27). It is another thing to understand what it means to live as fully renewed image bearers.

Our technological age, by design, does what it can to insulate or buffer us from the created order.[9] At the same time, helping teenagers embrace and affirm their creaturehood is rarely a significant ministry value. Historically, evangelism to youth assumed "bondage to sin" as its primary focus, often to the exclusion of creation and image bearing. This can unintentionally reduce conversion to a "commitment" or a prayer to be freed from bondage.

While this is a task of evangelism, it fails to appreciate the deep matter of human purpose found in the created order, and in the case of adolescents, the developmental task of identity.[10] Being able to articulate and demonstrate what freedom from bondage to sin and freedom into fully renewed image bearing looks like (the good life), according to the *telos* or trajectory of creation, is the key to contemporary evangelism to youth today.

We are created in God's image to "live and move and have our being" (Acts 17:28)—to *do things* that are consistent with those dynamics because as we do, not only do we find ourselves living a life of *shalom*, life the way it was meant to be (our theological mission), but we actually *become* what we were meant to be (our developmental mission).[11] The avenue into this theological and developmental mission includes three existential or lived-out dynamics from being created in the image of God. Adolescents were created for *allegiance, authority,* and *completing relationships*. Understanding each of these in their original intent and how they have been distorted by sin are the foundations to missional ministry, both theological and developmental.

First, adolescents are created to give themselves in *allegiance* to God because God is their creator, provider, and prohibitor (Genesis 2:7–9, 16), and loyalty to God is the means to discovering identity and worth. Another way to say this is that they were made with an impulse to *worship*.

Everyone worships, not just religious people. The only choice we have is *what* to worship. We all give ourselves, at any given moment, to someone or *something* outside ourselves, and teenagers are no exception. The critical part of this is that anything we give our allegiance to other than God ends up reshaping us in its image. Sin disrupts and distorts this worship impulse, persuading adolescents to give their allegiance to "lesser gods" (or *idols*) such as materialism, popularity, performance, or the demands of "saturated selves," etc. A life given to idols is a "lesser" life because one becomes like what one worships (Jeremiah 2:5; Psalm 115:3–8). Another way of saying this is "we become what we love."[12]

So instead of enjoying a flourishing life of worship where they discover intrinsic worth that begins to speak to their core questions of identity, adolescents struggle to know their true worth because they have given themselves to lesser things *that make them less*.

Second, adolescents are created with a kind of *authority* to bring justice and rightness to the world. God placed his image bearers in the Garden with a call and a capacity to be his agents that would move all created things forward in line with the trajectory of his wise order (Genesis 2:15).[13] Adolescents, and all humans, are authorized to make things right in the world around them.[14] This capacity is in line with their emerging autonomy, part of the normal adolescent journey, and is meant to be a kind of *authorization* to make things right (what the Bible often calls *righteousness*).

Sin disrupts this authorization and reorients it toward a misuse of power or oppression. As a result, disoriented teenagers live oppressing others and being oppressed themselves. This can range from sarcasm at the lunch table to exclusive cliques and clusters to destructive bullying and harassment. At the same time, they often feel *pressed* to conform to others' agendas, whether it is the pressures of school, to perform, to be recognized, or to conform to others' expectations (peers, teachers, parents, coaches).

They are vulnerable to these pressures and oppression because they long for what all adults long for—to know that their existence matters. Even for those who are not thinking about righteousness in a religious sense, they long to be a part of *rightness* because they long to know that they matter. Life never flourishes where there is any kind of misuse of authority because in an oppressive environment no one is using their authority for its intended purpose.[15]

Third, adolescents were created for *completing relationships* with others that generate a unique kind of dignity into their lives.[16] When Adam was introduced to Eve in Genesis 2:18–25, much took place, theologically and from a human relation standpoint. A larger view of this event shows God establishing a pattern for human relationships, according to the fixed nature of human beings created in his image, where an important portion of human identity is generated. When Adam said, "Bone of my bone and flesh of my flesh" in Genesis 2:23 (CSB), he affirmed that he had discovered something about who he was as a male and as a human through the presence of the female, Eve, that couldn't be discovered anywhere else in creation.

Because God chose to meet this dimension of identity through relationships with other humans, in essence, *community* and *belonging* become a part of the very fabric of the created order—they are interwoven and necessary to becoming a human person.[17] We simply can't be ourselves by ourselves, and relationships—properly understood in the biblical pattern—provide a human dignity that speaks identity into one another. "We act consistently with our dignity when we love God and our neighbor in the freedom given to us by God's love for us."[18]

As a result of being created in the image of God, adolescents have this impulse to *belong*, for profound relationships that shape who they are. This is particularly noteworthy at this stage of development. Adolescents are "expanding the field" of their significant relationships that contribute to their understanding of their identity from under the umbrella of family and out into the wider world of peers and nonparental adults.[19]

Because belonging is part of the created order, this means that all adolescent relationships, including opposite gender relationships, should be characterized by the *giving* of dignity. Unfortunately, the predominant, normative pattern for relationships in society is oriented toward consuming and exploiting others, not honoring others, nor giving them dignity.[20]

The unfortunate reality is that the pattern of relationships in the teenage world commonly encourages people to meet their own needs, often to the point of taking from others—even sexually—what does not belong to them. At some level, this is the root attraction of pornography—the impulse toward belonging and relating, distorted by sin and reduced to the exploitation of a two-dimensional human being. This also is the pattern of unhealthy dating relationships that hinge on personal sexual gratification disguised as love or affection.

Disordered relationships of all sorts *affect* adolescents (such as the fallout they experience from divorces, infidelity, abuse, and abandonment), and disordered relationships *infect* them (such as fallout from the dominant societal narrative that sexual activity is both inevitable and good, ignoring the fact that they are essentially consuming one another selfishly). No one becomes whole, especially teenagers, when their relationships are characterized by consuming one another.

Missional Ministry in Action: Bringing *Shalom* to Bear

Distorted versions of the theological longings are readily visible in adolescents. The painful realities in their lives often seem overwhelming to those who minister to them. This is only the eclipse, however. God's grand story, bringing his kingdom to bear in the world, can and will rewrite the dominant story of the day that seeks to normalize a dehumanizing way of life for adolescents. Jesus is the means into this re-humanizing and restoring story through his work on the cross.

The life of an adolescent today is *disintegrative*—that is, on a path toward fragmentation and incompleteness. Missional ministry, in order to intersect with adolescents developmentally and theologically and in order to speak into the brokenness and disintegration of their lives, needs to be more than a formula or a method. It needs to be *integrative*—intentionally committed to wholeness, flourishing, peace, and delight. In a word, *shalom*.

Remaining true to the *missio Dei* and its roots in the image of God, as well as its fruit, *shalom*, the three big ideas that should guide missional ministry practices are theological longings, developmental longings, and our kingdom/distorted longings. Figure 3 depicts the target we aim for in missional ministry.

Missional Ministry's Context: Shaping "Mini" Sacred Canopy

In the 1960s, sociologist Peter Berger suggested that belief in any real values, especially religious values, is only sustained in an environment where there are *plausibility structures* in place—institutions and common ground within society that support the same kinds of values, beliefs, and attitudes—what he called a sheltering or "sacred canopy."[21] For a great deal of the twentieth century, the West enjoyed a cultural and civic sacred canopy that was essentially in line with Judeo-Christian values and beliefs. That sacred canopy has eroded over the past few generations. As a result, much less in societal and cultural values sustain commitments to Christ.

Now, more than ever, teenagers need to see, feel, taste, and experience the realities of the gospel as well as hear the truth about Jesus. This means they need to see people who are committed to living out the richness of the *missio Dei*, the fullness of *shalom*, where the pervading ethos is that adolescents belong here, worship here, and are part of the action here. It also means thinking beyond the stand-alone youth group

Missional ministry to adolescents needs to converge around:
- Their theological longings—where is Jesus bearing witness to life the way it was meant to be?
- Their deep (developmental) longings—where is Jesus affirming, validating, or meeting those longings?
- Their distorted longings—where is Jesus standing against the distorted trajectory of the image of God?

God's Kingdom:
(Image of God Dynamics)

Theological Longings

Worship . . . Worth

Authority . . . Rightness

Relationships . . . Dignity

Renewed Relationship with God

Our Kingdom:
(Distortions of the Image of God)

Distorted Longings

Idolatries

Oppression

Exploitation

Distorted View of Self/Others

Adolescent Longings:

Developmental Longings

Who am I? (Identity)

To matter (Autonomy)

To fit in (Belonging)

Figure 3

and taking on the challenge to create a missional community or a "mini sacred canopy" to sustain and nurture faith.[22]

Adolescents grow up in a pluralistic society, with a marketplace of ideas. All the possibilities of belief, mediated through their technologies, help them shape their perception of reality. To borrow from Peter Berger again, the possibility of conversion—changing the way one perceives essential reality—is opened up through *encounters* with people who live with a contrasting view of reality. A person adopts and internalizes the new worldview through *resocialization* into a community sharing that new worldview.[23] Missional ministry assumes this mini sacred canopy, the local body of the church, is the countercultural setting best suited to shape adolescent worship rightly, aiming authority and power toward rightness and ordering relationships toward dignity. As in the days of the early church, it won't do to only talk about a "new life in Christ" to teenagers; you must be able to say, "Come join us and *experience* for yourself this new life in Christ, this *shalom* life as we live it in front of you, so you participate *in it* and are transformed by the renewing, maturing work of God toward the very end that you know in your bones you were made for.[24]

We, as redeemed, transformed, *shalom*-bearing followers of Jesus, should seriously consider this call, this mission, and the absolute necessity of our times, to create our own mini sacred canopy, our missional community, so we can invite others, especially youth, into this sort of life *with us*, so they can have the space and place to encounter authentic reality rooted in and committed to ministry practices that restore the image of God within them, bearing the fruit of *shalom* so that theologically and developmentally they can answer the question, "Who am I?"

Conclusion

The endpoint for missional ministry is integration into the body of Christ and the mission of Christ. This designation is another way of saying *wholeness*. The task of making adolescents whole means taking seriously their developmental needs (answering the question, "Who am I?") as well as their theological needs. Using the biblical lens of the image of God as a guide for missional ministry to youth allows ministry to be theological and developmental at the same time.

The quest to understand "Who am I?" is more than a psychosocial quest. Every developmental task in adolescence can trace its origins to theological roots: the quest to know what it means to have allegiances properly aligned, to have authority oriented toward rightness, and to have relationships that generate dignity.

The deep longings of this quest are met in Jesus today, because they are the same deep longings of the people he encountered when he lived and breathed and walked the earth. They may appear different in a new historical and social context, but they are the same at the core because they come from the same root: the *imago Dei* implanted in all people throughout all of history. If we listen well, we'll see these longings. If we earn trust, we can address these longings in the person and work of Jesus, as well as help youth see the ways they've redirected those dynamics of God's image in dehumanizing ways, so they can truly know life the way it was meant to be and become fully formed and *whole* followers of Jesus.

How Did We Get Here?

A Brief History of Christian Education and the Emergence of Youth Ministry

by Mark A. Maddix

● ● ● ● ● ● ● ● ● ● ● ● ●

Introduction

Why a history of youth ministry? What are the benefits of learning about facts, dates, and events that may seem irrelevant to youth ministry today? These are the typical questions raised when people study about history. History can often be perceived as irrelevant and disconnected from the realities of life today. However, history provides a narrative and rhythm of the changing theological and sociological landscape throughout the centuries.

In exploring history, we are able to see the fundamental shifts in how movements develop and their implications for ministry today. Any review of history raises the problem of organizing the efforts of Christian education into particular eras. The history of the church has several marker events or periods that have assisted other theorists writing about Christian education.[1] With several strong historical overviews already existing, this chapter provides a brief chronology of the dominant eras of Christian education and the emergence and growth of youth ministry as a distinct ministry focus.

Historical Foundations of Education

Old Testament Era

The children of Israel were nomadic people who lived amid other larger cultures, escaping from slavery and establishing a monotheistic nation in the midst of polytheistic practices, while maintaining a distinct identity and heritage.[2] The Hebrews engaged in various rituals such as religious ceremonies and festivals as Israel became a nation with a temple and a formal system of worship.

Later, during the exile, the family would return to the center of religious life and practice. By the beginning of the New Testament time, both family and synagogue collaborated as communities with specific stories, rituals, and festivals to guide formation within shifting contexts.

Religious education finds it roots in Hebrew education of the Old Testament. The *Shema* (Deuteronomy 6:4–5, ESV), "Hear, O Israel: The LORD our God, the LORD is one. You shall love the LORD your God with all your heart and with all your soul and with all your might," was the heart of the Torah. The goal of the Hebrew people was to love God and to love their neighbor.

The *Shema* was the measure by which the Hebrews were evaluated, even in the midst of keeping of the law. Therefore, Hebrew education had both a personal and communal faith dimension. It included relationship with God and relationship with others.[3] So to ensure that the *Shema* was central to the community, education took place first in the home. Parents, as well as other family members, were responsible to educate the children (Proverbs 1:8; 6:20), creating an intergenerational context for Hebrew education (Deuteronomy 4:9–11; 11:19–20). The socialization of children into the Hebrew community life, centered on the teaching of the Torah, provided a strong emphasis on the education and nurturing of the family.

For the Hebrews, learning (*lamath*) implied a subjective assimilation of the truths being learned and integration of those truths into life

(Deuteronomy 31:12–13). Learning was to be demonstrated in two ways: by a change of attitude and a change in action. The teacher's primary role was to instruct the Israelites in the Torah, so they would be viewed as a people set apart to serve God. Thus, learning was more about action than about just knowing information. To learn means to be transformed and to change a person's behavior.

Later in the history of Israel education took place in the synagogues, where the psalter was used and the Torah was read and interpreted. This combination of worship and religious instruction was a powerful means to preserve Hebrew culture and values. Through this process, the development of the teacher (rabbi) became elevated to the highest level in the community.

Israel's history is marred by disobedience to God and their desire to follow other gods. The prophets warned about their disobedience and neglect of Yahweh. As a result, Judah fell to the Babylonians in 586 B.C. Israel's religious life broke down because of a breakdown in its educational system. Because of their lack of obedience to the *Shema,* God disciplined his people. This is a good reminder that no education system is above the people working in it. If the teachers and leaders do not fear the Lord and delight in him, the best educational systems can fail (Jeremiah 2:5–8).

The beginning of Jewish education began with the close of the Hebrew period of Old Testament history. After the fall of Judah and the destruction of Jerusalem, the capital of Judah, the people of God, known as Jews (from Judea), were dispersed throughout the Mediterranean world. The dispersal patterns of Jewish communities were later called Diaspora.

After the exile, the prophet Ezra called Israel back to the Torah to ensure that history would not repeat itself. But Ezra and his followers became overly zealous in keeping the law, and a religious group or sect emerged called the Pharisees. They were concerned with strictly keeping the law. This movement prevailed during the four hundred years of the intertestamental period until the days of Jesus's ministry.

New Testament Era

Education processes in the New Testament and early church eras drew heavily from both Jewish and Greek cultures. With the rise of Greek education, a new formative emphasis stressed *padeia* (teaching) for the sake of citizenship. Greeks placed considerable emphasis on the city-state, and education shaped the leaders who governed the cities. Schools were developed to teach literature and philosophy—and to create good citizens. Greek education also sought to assist youth in the pursuit of virtues such as truth, fidelity, beauty, and goodness.[4] Greek education prepared citizens for global engagement as the empire expanded. They were to expand the influence of Greek culture and thought.

However, another form of transformation occurred through the life and ministry of Jesus. Jesus's engagement, teaching, and compassionate care modeled a different empire and kingdom that also prepared its citizens to engage the world. Jesus came to usher in a new kingdom and to invite followers to a life in a new faith community that modeled a different kingdom through proclamation and compassion.[5]

Jesus spent much of his ministry of teaching in response to the Pharisees and their view of the Torah. Jesus's message of repentance was a call back to the heart of the Torah, the *Shema*. This is reflected when Jesus was asked what was the greatest commandment. He responded by quoting the *Shema* (Matthew 22:36–40). Jesus was the master teacher, a rabbi, who was concerned about meeting the needs of the people and to bring the "good news to the poor. . . . freedom for the prisoners and recovery of sight for the blind, to set the oppressed free" (Luke 4:18). Jesus's message was rooted in a deep understanding of the Old Testament scriptures and a call to follow the heart of the Torah.

Jesus left his twelve disciples (and us) with the imperative of the great commission to go and "make disciples" (Matthew 28:19). The call of disciple-making is central to the process of Christian education and the overall mission of the church. Jesus reminds us that we are to teach them "everything I have commanded" (v. 20).

As followers of Christ begin to live out the message of Christ, they were called people of "the Way," and this new church movement began to grow. As the apostle Paul took the gospel to the Gentile world, he developed churches and wrote letters to address the growing needs of these congregations. Paul, a converted Jew, was both an evangelist and an educator who taught about the mysteries of Christ. As a result of his teaching, Christianity grew throughout Asia Minor.

As the church began to grow, there became a need for Christian education and nurture. Even though the early church was governed politically by Rome, Greek thought governed it intellectually and culturally. The education and teaching of the early church was influenced by the development of Greek culture and thought.

For example, consider the development of schools where formal education took place and where the teacher was a "spiritual father" of learners. In this regard, the Greek view of education was similar to the Jewish idea of a rabbi. Both recognized the importance of learning through the teacher and to imitate the life of the teacher. This kind of teaching resulted in a more static, receptive listening, rather than a firsthand experience with reality. The goal of education was to produce an active, creative, and independent person, whereas Roman education was more practical and concrete and addressed the realities of real life.

Early Church Era

During the first four centuries of the early church, one of the most important contributions of Christian education was the notion of the essential quality of every person. The church, like the state, acknowledged the necessity to educate everyone. The church leaders followed the Hebraic idea of educating the children in the home and realized the need to educate adults because of the threat of heresy and persecution of Christians. For those entering the church it meant weighing the serious consequence of becoming identified as a Christian. As a result, a catechetical process was developed to educate Christians about the life, death, burial, and resurrection of Jesus. The emphasis on education included *kerygma* (proclamation), which is the announcement of the gospel that encompasses a threefold theme of Christ's death, burial, and resurrection appearances.

The teacher was the one who heard, announced, and proclaimed the gospel message. And the *Didache* (teaching) was both a concept and a document in early religious education that developed a number of steps in the direction of creedal formulation. The teaching ministry of the church included both *kerygma* and *Didache* as essential aspects of Christian education. During the third century, a catechumenate system was developed to educate children and families as a means to integrate them into the church. It was designed to prepare members morally and spiritually for church membership. In essence, it was an integration process and membership training for new believers.

Catechesis stood not only for instruction but also for evangelism. During persecutions, the witness of the church stretched to include the martyrdom of early Christians, which often shaped the church's self-understanding of public evangelism.[6]

The Established Church Era

From the early church through the Middle Ages marks the longest Christian era. This era began with Constantine's incorporation of the church into Roman culture and ended with the divisions of the church—first the Greek Orthodox and Roman churches and finally the Reformation. This period resembled the church as the center of power (Roman and during the Middle era) and the margins of power (after the empires of Rome and Constantinople fell). Whatever the challenges, Christian education often served the church by preserving and perpetuating Christian thought in the midst of changing historical forces.[7]

Just after the fall of the Roman Empire, monastic orders were developed. The orders preserved the faith through disciplined living and daily devotions, serving the formative presence of the church in the midst of despair or during periods of excess in the Middle Ages. Monasteries served as locations for preservation of Scripture and theology during the collapse of Rome.[8]

Also, as the church grew throughout the Western world, cathedral schools provided basic leadership education in key areas of church law, doctrine, and church governance. They later gave way to the rise of universities, where the academic studies focused on theology as the "queen of the sciences." Cathedrals stood in the center of towns, providing needed services and guidance. Entire villages and regions embraced a church that influenced almost every aspect of personal life.

Coming out of the Middle Ages, the Renaissance ushered in the great intellectual awakening of the modern era. Unfortunately, this awakening was a missed opportunity for Christian education, where faith instruction faded behind the invention of the modern universities. A humanistic worldview replaced human reason in the position of ultimate authority and gave rise to an educational philosophy that focused solely on the acquisition of knowledge.[9]

The Reformation Era

The Reformation was marked by a growing distrust in the humanistic teaching of the Renaissance. In the desire to reform the church, Martin Luther, John Calvin, and others challenged the Christian faith with diverse, emerging traditions that demanded a fresh approach to Christian education.[10] Calvin emphasized the educational responsibility of the church and developed a philosophy of teaching for lifestyle transformation rather than simply for the acquisition of knowledge. Luther focused on the educational responsibility of the home, the centrality of Scripture, and education of all boys and girls. Basic catechisms were written to be used in churches or in the homes, including Martin

Luther's "Table Talks," *The Westminster Catechism,* and the Anglican Church's "Articles of Religion."[11]

As the new church developed, it was faced with creating new traditions and practices, including the Lord's Supper, with specific church practices. New prayers and prayer books were written, along with devotional guides. The printing press provided a powerful tool to establish a more universal education. As education spread, the role of teaching grew as a powerful tool to expand the new movement. For example, in England this marked the rise of the Anglican, Catholic, and Puritan influence on the religious and educational landscape for nearly two hundred years.

The Modern Church, Eighteenth and Nineteenth Century

The Enlightenment of the eighteenth century shaped the modern church. Disillusioned by the Enlightenment, which focused on knowledge rather than on religious authority, a new emphasis on religious experience (also known as Pietism) and childhood education emerged. The influence of progressive educators such as in Jean Jacques Rousseau's book, *Emile,* focused on the individual experience of the child through play and experiential learning. Others such as John Amos Comenius, Johannes Pestalozzi, and Friedrich Froebel (founder of the kindergarten), provided educational avenues for children to learn about the world through their senses. Early educational efforts in the United States included the creation of the Mc-Guffey Reader, which shaped a generation of young learners.[12]

Religious experience provided a powerful formative influence during the great awakenings of the eighteenth and nineteenth centuries, characterized by the revival movements of John and Charles Wesley and Charles Whitefield. The movements were shaped by altar calls and individual religious experiences. During this great awakening, several endeavors were established for the education of children and youth.

Sunday School Movement

In 1780, Robert Raikes, a man of moderate wealth and champion of the poor, determined that educating delinquent children could curb their voice of degeneration. He started the first Sunday school in Gloucester, England, with the primary objective of literacy training. But children were also given some Christian education as they were taught to read the Bible, memorize catechisms, and attend worship.[13] The Sunday school movement spread to the United States by the efforts of William Elliot, who opened a Sunday school on the frontier of Virginia in 1785. The American Sunday School Union was established in 1824 to plant Sunday schools through the Mississippi Valley. The result was over 30,000 professions of faith in the Mississippi Valley. The American Sunday School Union was comprised of local Sunday school "unions" who brought Sunday school workers together for encouragement and training at the "union" meetings.[14]

Also, in 1859, Dwight Moody, from Chicago, established Sunday schools that focused on evangelism. Following the Civil War, Moody and a group of men known as the Illinois Band transformed the Sunday school movement into a mission of evangelical Protestantism.[15]

Young Men's Christian Association (YMCA)

The Young Men's Christian Association (YMCA) was founded by George Williams in England in 1844 and was introduced to America in 1851, followed by the Young Women's Christian Association in 1858. The early years of the YMCA were closely associated with revival movements and evangelism efforts. A Presbyterian pastor, Theodore Culyer, conceived of a prayer meeting for youth that would perpetuate the prayer revival tied to the YMCA in 1857–59. The YMCA also influenced nineteenth-century youth ministry because it chose to train leaders in training schools rather than in union gatherings. The model of training more closely paralleled youth ministry education in the last quarter of the twentieth century.[16]

Over time, as the YMCA expanded its operations and formulated training schools into colleges, core evangelical doctrines gave way to a more liberal theological perspective.[17] Many of the YMCA and YWCA today do not reflect its original beginnings but are more ecumenical in focus and less evangelical.

Christian Nurture and Horace Bushnell

As the revival movement of the eighteenth century grew and as organizations such as the Sunday school and the YMCA engaged in evangelical efforts, another movement that focused on Christian nurture would rock the church and forever change the landscape of Christian education.

Horace Bushnell was a pastor and wrote prolifically on topics such as Christian nurture, naturalism, and supernaturalism.[18] While he attended Yale, Bushnell was converted during the 1831 revival. After he graduated in 1833, he became the pastor of North Congregational church in Hartford, Connecticut, where he served until 1859.[19] During the first years of his pastorate he tried to recreate the spirit of the Yale revival—to discouraging results. So he rejected revivalism and turned to a theology of Christian nurture placing emphasis "that a child would grow up Christian and never know himself as being otherwise."[20]

In his book *Christian Nurture* (1861), Bushnell argued that instead of raising a child to be converted at a later date, which was the prevalent practice at that time, Christian parents should raise their children from their earliest days to love God and to follow his ways.[21] He combated the revivalist by arguing that the aim of Christian education in the home was to nurture Christian lifestyle and faith as a normal way of life.

For Bushnell, being a Christian involved not so much a dramatic decision but a process of formation. He viewed this "organic connection" as an integral part of human experience.

Bushnell's theory of Christian nurture became influential in the twentieth-century religious education movement through the influence of progressive educators such as George Albert Coe, C. Ellis Nelson,

John Westerhoff III, and Lawrence O. Richards. Each of these theorists grounded their theories of Christian education on a socialization approach to formation that takes place through parents and the faith community.

The Emergence of Youth Ministry

As the dawn of the twentieth century emerged, so did a new sociological phenomenon that created the concept called adolescence.[22] In 1904, G. Stanley Hall, the father of adolescent research, published the book *Adolescence*. The book marks the beginning of a systematic exploration, both empirically and theoretically, of adolescence as a life stage. Hall depicted adolescence as a tumultuous period, a havoc caused by raging hormones brought about by puberty.

Up to this point in human history there were two distinct stages of development, childhood and adulthood. But with the decline in the average age of puberty for women from fifteen a century ago to eleven or under at the turn of the century, a new stage was developed. Today adolescence can be defined as the period between puberty (biology) and finding one's place in the world (sociology).

Along with the regression of the age of puberty came the rise of the minimum legal age of marriage from twelve to eighteen in the United States. Also, in 1875, the United States Supreme Court allowed tax money to be spent on high school education. This move assured that, in time, nearly all young people would extend their adolescence from puberty through high school graduation.[23]

The beginning of youth ministry is hard to establish, but given the sociological shifts of youth and the creation of a new stage of development called adolescence, most Christian educators state that the beginning of the youth ministry movement began with the Society for Christian Endeavor.

The Society for Christian Endeavor

During this sociological shift of adolescence and the influence of Bushnell's Christian nurture, Francis E. Clark started the Society for Christian Endeavor on February 2, 1881. Clark was the pastor of Williston Church in Portland, Maine. He and his wife, Harriet, were looking for a way to assist young people of their congregation to continue their Christian faith after an initial salvation experience.[24] Clark responded to the concern of many pastors that true conversion had not taken place in the lives of young people because they seemed to disregard reverence for the Sabbath and the restraints of the principles of Christian religion. Also fueling the discussion was the growing influence of Bushnell, which questioned the idea of a dramatic conversion experience for children raised in Christian homes.[25]

Christian Endeavor redefined spirituality for youth by taking the following pledge:

Trusting in the Lord God Jesus Christ for strength, I promise Him I will try to do whatever He would have me do; that I will pray to Him and read my Bible every day, and that, just so far as I know how, through my whole life I will try to lead a Christian life.[26]

Active members between the ages of thirteen and thirty were required to sign the pledge, unlike associate members who were unwilling to call themselves Christians but were interested in the fellowship and activities. As Mark Senter III wrote,

The pledge provided a formula for youthful spirituality shared across denominations in America. Elastic enough to assume either a conversion experience or Bushnell's understanding that children raised in the faith community could grow up never thinking of themselves as anything but Christian, the point of the pledge was to continuously foster the work of Christ in the life of youthful believers. It had to do with Christian Spirituality.[27]

In essence, Christian Endeavor combined both Christian nurture (for those who were Christian) and missional engagement (for those who were seeking faith).

Also during this time a variety of other club activities followed, such as the Boys Club of America (1906), 4-H Clubs (1907), Camp Fire Girls (1910), Boys Scouts of America (1910), and Girls Scouts of America (1912). These clubs shared a Judeo-Christian value system but were not necessarily religious in nature.

Summary

The impact of Christian Endeavor and some of these other organizations were greatly influenced by the progressive education movement and liberal theology, which impacted youth work. Youth gatherings became dominated by topics of stewardship, social issues, and denominational distinctives, rather than by the proclamation of the gospel and the study of Scripture.

As the twentieth century approached, liberal theology and progressive education offered youth ministry a departure from nineteenth-century evangelism and piety. By the 1920s and 1930s, the goals of youth ministry in mainline churches had become indistinguishable from the goals of professional educators and public education—a realm indifferent to the influence of Christian theology.[28] For the most part, volunteer youth workers and church leaders outside of mainline Protestantism did not accept the theoretical shift from evangelicalism and piety to liberal theology and progressive education.[29] The influence of World War I illustrated the downfall of liberal assumptions that education would prove the key to improving civilization. As a result, evangelical youth ministry began to develop some avenues to reach youth for Christ.

The Rise of Evangelical Youth Movements

The rise of the evangelical movement[30] can be traced to Herbert J. Taylor (1893–1978) and his wife, Gloria, who founded a mission during the Great Depression on the north side of Chicago. They wanted to provide organizations and people who could reach unchurched children and youth and direct them to the church.[31] Taylor was president of Club Aluminum Products Company and was ready to finance organizations to reach the unchurched people of America. Taylor, a Methodist layperson, did not turn to the church but to interdenominational agencies such as Youth for Christ, Young Life, and Inter-Varsity to provide financial support and to advance the gospel.[32]

Youth for Christ

The origins of Youth for Christ are almost impossible to trace. The movement had no founder; it had an explosion. This explosion began in 1904 by young evangelists in Great Britain, Frederick and Arthur Wood, who set out to preach the gospel to Great Britain. After several years of ministry, they realized that most of their converts were young people. In 1911, they began a series of *Young Life* Campaigns (not to be confused with the Young Life organization) through Great Britain and reached thousands of young people.[33]

Probably the first youth rally director in America was the fiery Lloyd Bryant. He organized weekly rallies in the early 1930s and is considered the founder of Youth for Christ. He modeled his ministry after the *Young Life* Campaign in England and reached millions of unchurched young people.

Also, in 1933 Evelyn McClusky established the Miracle Book Club in Portland, Oregon, which by 1938 had planted more than one thousand clubs across the country.[34] McClusky clubs attracted people into leadership positions, and those people went on to significantly impact the Youth for Christ movement. One of those was Jim Rayburn, who established the Young Life organization.

With the rise of the Youth for Christ movement in the 1930s and 1940s, evangelical Christians sought to revitalize youth ministry, especially since many Protestant youth ministry organizations had become liberal and were in decline. The Youth for Christ organization gained national visibility because of youth evangelists like Percy Crawford, Jim Rayburn, Torrey Johnson, and Billy Graham.

On July 22, 1945, forty-two delegates met at Winona Lake, Indiana, to found Youth for Christ International. Torrey Johnson, the president of the National Association of Evangelicals, recruited Billy Graham as the first full-time evangelist for the movement. The combination of Youth for Christ and the NAE focused on evangelistic mission through large rallies in auditoriums and stadiums. Youth for Christ thrived under Johnson's leadership and through the preaching of Billy Graham. In just two years Graham preached in forty-seven of the forty-eight states and throughout Canada. He developed a friendship with a team of young men who, in time, emerged as the nucleus of the Billy Graham Evangelistic Association.[35]

The development of the Youth for Christ movement and the development of evangelicalism through the NAE cannot be separated. This is where the theological roots of youth evangelism were developed, in stark contrast to the theology of nurture in youth ministry founded by Christian Endeavor.[36] Some argue that this evangelical resurgence by Billy Graham and the NAE was the "fourth great awakening" in America. The influence of evangelicalism shaped the common core of beliefs in American history and culture.

Young Life

Unlike Youth for Christ, which seemed to explode, Young Life was the result of the vision of one young man, Jim Rayburn. Rayburn was a Presbyterian minister who was disillusioned with the traditional church and had a gift for reaching high school students. In the fall of 1938 he started the Miracle Club in Gainesville, Texas. The club met once a week after school, but it was disappointing. He decided to spend Friday and Saturday nights watching ball games and hanging around high school students. He then moved his high school club to an evening hour at his home. The club exploded, and he developed the basic principles of Young Life that are still prevalent today:

1. Hold meetings with teenagers away from school. They are more comfortable in homes than they are in school or in church. Teenagers will go where their friends are.

2. Aim for leaders in the school; others will follow.

3. Make the meeting enjoyable: skits, jokes, and singing.

Young Life was built on developing relationship with teens and meeting with them in homes. To this day, Young Life evangelism focuses on a network of personal relationships as a means of evangelism.[37]

InterVarsity Christian Fellowship

InterVarsity began at the University of Cambridge in 1877 when students met to pray, to study the Bible, and to witness to fellow students. The groups spread throughout Great Britain and then to Canada. In 1938, Stacey Woods, the Canadian InterVarsity director, met with students on the University of Michigan campus to form the first chapter of IVF in America. In 1941 InterVarsity Christian Fellowship/USA was organized with three staff and Stacey Woods at the helm as secretary general. By 1950, there were nearly five hundred chapters across the country, and InterVarsity started to supply literature for the ministry.[38]

Growth of Parachurch Ministries and Christian Camping

The growth of evangelicalism through Youth for Christ, the National Association of Evangelicals, Young Life, and InterVarsity Fellowship helped to shape the landscape of youth ministry in local congregations and many denominations. With the focus on evangelistic youth rallies and large events, relational-based youth ministry set the stage for the next generation of youth ministry and the growth of various parachurch ministries, such as Youth for Christ (1944), Fellowship of Christian Athletes (1954), Campus Crusade for Christ (1951), and Youth with a Mission (1960).

As these parachurch ministries grew through youth rallies and Saturday night extravaganzas, camps and retreat centers developed to minister to youth. For example, in 1946 Young Life bought a ranch near Pikes Peak, Colorado, called Star Ranch. Camping ministries expanded in many denominations and club programs modeled after scouting were developed, such as the Christian Service Brigade (1937), Pioneer Girls (1939), and AWANA (1950). In 1934, the Church of the Nazarene, under the leadership of Leroy Haynes, developed a club program that focused on scouting, which developed into the Caravan program in the 1940s.[39]

Youth Ministry Expansion

The growth of youth ministry during the first half of the twentieth century gave rise to the establishment of youth ministry as a profession, both in parachurch- and congregational-based ministries. During the latter half of the century, various professional youth ministry organizations developed to address the growing demand for youth leaders and pastors.

Probably the most dominant of these was Youth Specialties, founded in 1969 by Wayne Rice and Mike Yaconelli. Rice and Yaconelli were youth pastors who set out to convince pastors and local congregations that they needed to take youth ministry seriously and that it could be relevant and fun. They developed the first annual Youth Specialties National Youth Workers Convention in 1970 to train and equip youth workers and pastors. Youth Specialties caught the attention of Zondervan publishing in 1974 and began producing resources for youth workers and teenagers.[40]

The influence of Youth Specialties shaped the landscape of youth ministry in America, particularly congregational youth ministry. Other youth ministry organizations developed during this time such as Son City (1968) led by Bill Hybels and Dave Holmbo; Sonlife Ministries

(1979) by Dann Spader; Group, Inc. by Thom Schultz (1974); and the National Network of Youth Ministries (1979) by Paul Fleischmann.

Current Developments in Youth Ministry

The establishment of parachurch ministries such as Young Life, Youth for Christ, and Youth Specialties was largely due to local congregations not focusing on the evangelism of youth. But current developments in youth ministry have come full circle as denominations have developed a theology of youth ministry that is grounded in local congregations. This focus places youth ministry in the broader framework of practical theology and frees youth ministry from the predominate influences of the social sciences.[41] It also has provided a way for mainline denominations with declining attendance to rethink the role of the church in nurturing and evangelizing youth. The leading voices today are youth ministry educators such as Kenda Creasy Dean, professor of practical theology at Princeton Theological Seminary; Chap Clark, pastor at St. Andrews Presbyterian Church in Newport Beach (former professor of practical theology at Fuller Theological Seminary); and David Rahn, professor of youth ministry at Huntington University. In their book, *Starting Right: Thinking Theologically about Youth Ministry* (2001), the authors root youth ministry in theological foundations of ecclesiology and the local church. Dean, Clark, and Rahn focus on the role parents, mentors, and local congregations play in forming teenagers' faith. Also, Kara Powell (Fuller Theological Seminary) and Chap Clark have developed a practical theology that integrates theology and the social sciences.[42] Their work has encouraged a greater focus on intergenerational youth ministry, which focuses on the role of imitation and modeling for faith formation. Their book, *Sticky Faith: Everyday Ideas to Build Lasting Faith in Your Kids* (2011), points to the role parents have in shaping faith formation. These efforts have led to the development of several other youth ministry educators' theological grounding of youth ministry, such as Andrew Root, a Lutheran who grounds youth ministry in a relational Christology.[43]

Another recent development in youth ministry has been the influence of Rick Warren, pastor of Saddleback Church in Lake Forest, California. Warren's book *The Purpose-Driven Church* (1995) influenced many congregations' views of discipleship. His youth pastor, Doug Fields, wrote *Purpose-Driven Youth Ministry* (1998), which built on Warren's approach to discipleship and leadership development. Fields's book focused on developing youth discipleship and creating a healthy youth ministry, which impacted many congregationally based youth ministries. Fields's approach provided a youth ministry framework to educate disciples and to reach unchurched youth.

These recent developments in youth ministry are shaping the landscape in congregations and parachurch organizations. Their impact on the history of youth ministry is yet to be seen, but the initial results indicate that it will help ground youth ministry in a broader theological framework of the church, particularly as it relates to forming faith and engaging in mission in the world.

Conclusion

The history of Christian education has strong foundations in Scripture. The Hebraic emphasis of the role of the family and the synagogue as the primary avenue to pass on the faith and to shape the next generation is a model of how faith formation takes place. In the New Testament the life and teachings of Jesus provided the early church with a model of how to engage in acts of compassion and service to others. The early church created catechetical processes to educate families about the life, death, and resurrection of Jesus Christ. The combination of *kerygma* and *Didache* became central to the growth of the church. As the church emerged through the Middle Ages, the monastic order preserved Scripture and theology, and the Enlightenment gave rise to intellectual pursuits and the development of academic centers, cathedrals, and educational philosophy. In reaction to the Enlightenment, the Reformers moved Scripture back to the center and provided Christian education for all children, including placing Christian education back in the parents' hands.

As revivalism grew, there was a greater focus on pietism and personal development. The contrast between revivalism and the Christian nurture of Horace Bushnell became evident as Christian education took place in America. The focus on Christian nurture became evident in such organizations as Christian Endeavor and the YMCA. The growth of clubs established more liberal theology as the norm among many parachurch organizations and mainline congregations. In reaction, the evangelical youth ministry movement rose with the impact of Youth Life, Youth for Christ, and InterVarsity Christian Fellowship. Rallies and crusades, along with the NAE, brought evangelical youth ministry back to the front of American society and culture.

Camping ministries and professional youth workers' organizations, such as Youth Specialties, expanded youth ministry into the last half of the twentieth century. More contemporary approaches to youth ministry, grounded in a theology of the church, have become the primary focus of youth ministry educators. This includes a greater focus on intergenerational youth ministry and missional engagement in the world. In many ways, youth ministry has come full-circle from its beginnings to provide a context for teenage faith to be nurtured (Christian Endeavor) and a place where evangelism can take place in a local context (Young Life).

The combination of Christian nurture and evangelism makes youth ministry effective. Teenagers need faith communities to nurture their faith, and they need youth leaders who can communicate the gospel in the changing culture. The history of youth ministry reminds us that God continues to work through both local congregations and parachurch organizations to bring about the mission of the church and the establishment of God's kingdom.

Appendix A

• • • • • • • • • • • •

Sunday School Exchange #1

Suggested Plan

Note to teacher or leader: Thanks for your willingness to use this Sunday School Exchange! The primary objective today is getting to know each other and for each person to share a bit about themselves. Feel free to follow this guide.

I. Opening: Gathering and refreshments (if applicable)!

II. Introduction: This activity can be done in the large group or in small groups. Break into small groups with a mix (half and half) of adult and youth participants. Take time for each person to introduce themselves and to answer these questions:

1. Name

2. Grade/age and/or occupation

3. Favorite place to eat

4. What do you understand is the purpose of the Sunday School Exchange? (Or) Do you know why we are together today?

This could be a good time to explain that the purpose of gathering an adult class and a grade-level class together (Sunday School Exchange) is simply to meet and get to know other age groups in the church. You can add: "We believe there is great value in each other, but unless we plan opportunities (like this) it may never happen. So here we are!"

III. Table Talk: The Four Quaker Questions

1. Where did you live between the ages of five and twelve, and what were the winters like? (*Some people may have lived in several places, so tell them to choose one place.*)

2. How was your home heated?

3. Two parts:

   A. What was the center of warmth in your life when you were a child? (*This can be a place in the house, a time of year, or perhaps a person.*)

   B. Who was the center of warmth in your life? (*This is a person.*)

4. When did God become a "warm" being to you and how did this happen?

IV. Personal Testimony: If time allows ask for additional information about the current faith journey of one adult and one younger person. Perhaps use a question like, "Where have you seen God at work in your life over the past month?"

V. Prayer: Ask for prayer requests (at least one) from each person, and then take time to pray together. (Suggestions: Have each person pray for the person on their right or have adults pray for young people or have one person pray for the group.)

Appendix B

· · · · · · · · · · · · ·

Sunday School Exchange #2

Suggested Plan

Note to teacher or leader: Tell attendees: "Thanks for your involvement in our Sunday School Exchange! The primary objective today is getting to know each other's faith stories. Research, like the National Study of Youth and Religion, describes how meaningful it can be for young and old to share their faith stories with each other."

I. Opening: Gathering and refreshments (if applicable)

II. Introduction: This first activity can be done in the large group or in small groups. Break into small groups with a mix (half and half) of adult and youth participants. Take time for each person to introduce themselves and answer the following questions:

1. Name

2. Grade/age and/or occupation

3. Best vacation you've ever been on

4. What do you understand is the purpose of the Sunday School Exchange? (Or) Do you know why we are together today?

This could be a good time to explain that the purpose of gathering an adult class and a grade-level class together (Sunday School Exchange) is simply to meet and get to know other age groups in the church. You can add: "We believe there is great value in each other, but unless we plan opportunities (like this) it may never happen. So here we are!"

III. Table Talk: Faith Stories

1. If you have a personal relationship with Jesus Christ: What was your life like before meeting Jesus Christ? (Family, job, marriage, friends, etc.)

2. What circumstances surrounded the moment when you met Jesus Christ? (Summer camp, at bedside with a parent, or other?)

3. Describe to the group what life with Christ is like for you since meeting Christ and how things are going currently. (Full, rich, lonely, desert time?)

IV. Personal Testimony: If time allows, ask for additional information about the current faith journey of one adult and one younger person around the table. Perhaps ask a question like, "How have you seen God at work in your life over the past month?"

V. Prayer: Ask for at least one prayer request from each person, and then take time to pray together. (Suggestions: Have each person pray for the person on their right, have adults pray for young people, or have one person pray for the group.)

Bibliography

• • • • • • • • • • • •

Anchor Bible Dictionary. Vol. 1 (A-C). New York: Doubleday, 1992.

Anderson, Ray S. *The Shape of Practical Theology: Empowering Ministry with Theological Praxis.* Downer's Grove, IL: InterVarsity Press, 2001.

———. *The Soul of Ministry: Forming Leaders for God's People.* Louisville, KY: Westminster John Knox, 1997.

Arnett, Jeffrey Jensen. *Emerging Adulthood: The Winding Road from the Late Teens through the Twenties.* New York: Oxford University Press, 2004.

———. *Readings on Adolescence and Emerging Adulthood.* Upper Saddle River, NJ: Prentice Hall, 2002.

Augsburger, David. *Dissident Discipleship: A Spirituality of Self-Surrender, Love of God, and Love of Neighbor.* Grand Rapids: Brazos Press, 2006.

Berger, Peter L., and Thomas Luckmann. *The Social Construction of Reality: A Treatise in the Sociology of Knowledge.* 1st ed. Garden City, NY: Doubleday, 1966.

Black, David Alan. *The Myth of Adolescence: Raising Responsible Children in an Irresponsible Society.* Yorba Linda, CA: Davidson Press, 1999.

Black, Wesley. *An Introduction to Youth Ministry.* Nashville: Broadman, 1991.

Blevins, Dean G., and Mark A. Maddix. *Discovering Discipleship: Dynamics of Christian Education.* Kansas City: Beacon Hill Press of Kansas City, 2010.

Blos, Peter. *The Adolescent Passage: Developmental Issues.* New York: International Universities Press, 1979.

Bond, Stuart Cummings. "The One-Eared Mickey Mouse." *Youthworker* (Fall 1989).

Borgman, Dean. *When Kumbaya Is Not Enough: A Practical Theology for Youth Ministry.* Peabody, MA: Hendrickson Publishers, 1997.

Bronfenbrenner, Urie. *The Ecology of Human Development: Experiments by Nature and Design.* Cambridge, MA: Harvard University Press, 1979.

Brueggemann, Walter. *Genesis; Interpretation: Bible Commentary for Teaching and Preaching.* Boulder, CO: NetLibrary, 1982.

Burns, Jim, and Mike DeVries. *Partnering with Parents in Youth Ministry: The Practical Guide to Today's Family-Based Youth Ministry.* Ventura, CA: Gospel Light, 2003.

Bushnell, Horace. *Christian Nurture.* New York: Charles Scribner, 1961.

Ceci, Stephen J., and Wendy M. Williams, eds., *The Nature-Nurture Debate: The Essential Readings.* Malden, MA: Blackwell Publishers Ltd., 1999.

Christensen, Duane L. *Deuteronomy 1-11.* Vol. 6A of *Word Biblical Commentary.* Dallas: Word, 1991.

Clark, Chap. "Adolescent Development and Spiritual Formation." Course Description. Pasadena, CA: Fuller Theological Seminary, 2006.

———. "The Adoption View of Youth Ministry." In *Youth Ministry in the 21st Century.* Edited by Chap Clark. Grand Rapids: Baker Academic, 2015.

———. "The Changing Face of Adolescence: A Theological View of Human Development." In *Starting Right: Thinking Theologically about Youth Ministry.* Edited by Kenda Creasy Dean, Chap Clark, and David Rahn. Grand Rapids: Zondervan, 2001.

———. *Hurt: Inside the World of Today's Teenagers.* Youth, Family, and Culture. Edited by Chap Clark. Grand Rapids: Baker Academic, 2004.

———. *Hurt 2.0: Inside the World of Today's Teenagers.* Grand Rapids: Baker Academic, 2011.

Clark, Chap, and Kara E. Powell. *Deep Ministry in a Shallow World: Not-So-Secret Findings about Youth Ministry.* Grand Rapids: Zondervan, 2006.

Collins, Raymond F. *First Corinthians: Sacra Pagina.* Collegeville, MN: Liturgical Press, 1999.

Dahl, Ronald E., and Linda Patia Spear, eds. *Adolescent Brain Development: Vulnerabilities and Opportunities.* New York: New York Academy of Sciences, 2004.

Dean, Kenda Creasy. *Almost Christian: What the Faith of Our Teenagers Is Telling the American Church.* New York: Oxford, 2010.

———. *Practicing Passion: Youth and the Quest for a Passionate Church.* Grand Rapids: Eerdmans, 2004.

Dean, Kenda Creasy, and Ron Foster. *The Godbearing Life: The Art of Soul Tending for Youth Ministry.* Nashville: Upper Room Books, 1998.

Dettoni, John M. *Introduction to Youth Ministry.* Grand Rapids: Zondervan, 1993.

DeVries, Mark. *Family-Based Youth Ministry: Reaching the Been-There, Done-That Generation.* Downers Grove, IL: InterVarsity, 1994.

———. *Sustainable Youth Ministry: Why Most Youth Ministry Doesn't Last and What Your Church Can Do About It.* Downers Grove, IL: IVP, 2008.

DeVries, Mark, and Jeff Dunn-Rankin. *The Indispensable Youth Pastor: Land, Love, Lock in Your Youth Ministry Dream Job.* Colorado Springs, CO: Group, 2011.

Dougherty, Rose Mary. *Group Spiritual Direction: Community for Discernment.* New York: Paulist Press, 1995.

Downs, Perry. "Christian Nurture: A Comparison of Horace Bushnell and Lawrence O. Richards." *Christian Education Journal* 4, no. 2 (1983).

Drane, John. *Do Christians Know How to Be Spiritual? The Rise of New Spirituality and the Mission of the Church.* London: Darton, Longman, and Todd, 2005.

Drury, Keith. *The Call of a Lifetime: How to Know if God Is Leading You to the Ministry.* Indianapolis: Wesleyan, 2013.

Dunn, Richard. "What Are the Necessary Competencies to Be an Effective Youth Worker?" *Christian Education Journal* 16, no. 3 (1996): 25–38.

Elkind, David. *The Hurried Child: Growing Up Too Fast Too Soon.* 3rd ed. Cambridge, MA: Da Capo Press, 2007.

Epstein, Robert. *The Case Against Adolescence: Rediscovering the Adult in Every Teen.* Fresno, CA: Quill Driver Books, 2007.

Erikson, Erik H. *Identity and Life Cycle.* New York: W. W. Norton, 1980.

———. *Identity: Youth and Crisis.* New York: W. W. Norton, 1968.

Estep, James Riley, Jonathan Hyungsoo Kim, Alvin Wallace Kuest, and Mark Amos Maddix. *C.E.: The Heritage of Christian Education.* Joplin, MO: College Press, 2003.

Evans, David M. *Shaping the Church's Ministry with Youth.* Valley Forge, PA: Judson Press, 1965.

Feinberg, Walter. "For Goodness Sake: How Religious Stories Work to Make Us Good and the Goodness That They Make." *Studies in Philosophy and Education* 23, no. 1 (2004): 1–19.

Fields, Doug. *Purpose-Driven Youth Ministry: 9 Essential Foundations for Healthy Growth.* Grand Rapids: Zondervan, 1998.

Gladson, Jerry A. "Spiritual Direction, Social Justice, and the United Church of Christ." *Journal of Psychology and Theology* 30, no. 4 (2002): 346–54.

Goldingay, John. "Pentateuch." Class lecture at Fuller Theological Seminary, 2005.

Gollnick, James. *Religion and Spirituality in the Life Cycle.* New York: Peter Lang Publishing, 2005.

Gorman, Joe. *Healthy. Happy. Holy.: 7 Practices Toward a Holistic Life.* Kansas City: Beacon Hill Press of Kansas City, 2018.

Gossai, Hemchand. "Divine Evaluation and the Quest for a Suitable Companion." *Cross Currents* 52 (Winter 2004).

Grenz, Jonathan. "Factors Influencing Vocational Changes Among Youth Ministers." *Journal of Youth Ministry* 1, no. 1 (2002): 73–88.

Guder, Darrell L., ed. *Missional Church: A Vision for the Sending of the Church in North America*. Grand Rapids: Eerdmans, 1998.

Guenther, Margaret. *At Home in the World: A Rule of Life for the Rest of Us*. New York: Church Publishing, 2006.

Gula, Richard M. *The Good Life: Where Morality and Spirituality Converge*. New York: Paulist Press, 1999.

Guyon, Jeanne. *Experiencing the Depths of Jesus Christ*. Edited by Gene Edwards. Beaumont, TX: Seed Sowers, 1975.

Hagner, Donald A. *Matthew*. Vols. 33A and 33B of *Word Biblical Commentary*. Dallas: Word, 1993.

Hall, Douglas John. *Professing the Faith: Christian Theology in a North American Context*. Minneapolis: Fortress Press, 1996.

Hall, G. Stanley. *Adolescence: Its Psychology and Its Relations to Physiology, Anthropology, Sociology, Sex, Crime, Religion and Education*. New York: D. Appleton, 1904.

Hamilton, Stephen F., and Mary Agnes Hamilton. "School, Work, and Emerging Adulthood." *Emerging Adults in America: Coming to Age in the 21st Century*. Edited by Jeffrey Jensen Arnett and Jennifer Lynn Tanner. Washington, DC: American Psychological Association, 2006.

Hardwired to Connect: The New Scientific Case for Authoritative Communities. New York: Institute for American Values, 2003.

Hart, Archibald D. *Adrenaline and Stress*. Nashville: Thomas Nelson, 1995.

Hayford, Sarah R., and Frank F. Furstenberg Jr. "Delayed Adulthood, Delayed Desistance? Trends in the Age Distribution of Problem Behaviors." *Journal of Research on Adolescence* 18, no. 2 (2008): 285–304.

Hays, Richard B. *First Corinthians; Interpretation: A Bible Commentary for Teaching and Preaching*. Louisville, KY: John Knox, 1997.

Mark Hayse, *Youth Ministry, Obesity, and the Rhetorics of Faith*, unpublished paper presented at the 2012 Association of Youth Ministry Educators Conference, Dallas, TX, October 2012.

Highfield, Ron. *God, Freedom and Human Dignity: Embracing a God-Centered Identity in a Me-Centered Culture*. Downers Grove, IL: InterVarsity Press, 2013.

Hildebrand, Verna. *Parenting: Rewards and Responsibilities*. 8th ed. New York: McGraw-Hill, 2007.

Hine, Thomas. *The Rise and Fall of the American Teenager*. New York: Perennial Press, 1999.

Howard, Megan, and Jon Barrett, ed. *Teen People: Faith; Stories of Belief and Spirituality*. New York: Harper Collins, 2001.

Huntemann, Nina, and Michael Morgan. "Mass Media and Identity Development." In *Handbook of Children and the Media*. Edited by Dorothy G. Singer and Jerome L. Singer. Thousand Oaks, CA: Sage Publishing, 2001.

Hunter, George, III. *The Celtic Way of Evangelism: How Christianity Can Reach the West . . . Again*. Nashville: Abingdon Press, 2000.

Jack, Andrew S., and Barrett W. McRay. "Tassel Flipping: A Portrait of the Well-Educated Youth Ministry Graduate." *Journal of Youth Ministry* 4, no. 1 (2005): 53–74.

Jewett, Paul King, and Marguerite Shuster. *Who We Are: Our Dignity as Human; A Neo-Evangelical Theology*. Grand Rapids: Eerdmans, 1996.

Jones, Kathryn Croskery. "Obstacles to Accountability." *Journal of Religion and Abuse* 6, no. 1 (2004): 37–45.

Jones, Timothy Paul, ed. *Perspectives on Family Ministry: Three Views*. Nashville: B&H Academic, 2009.

Jung, Carl G. *Personality Types*. Princeton, NJ: Princeton University Press, 1971.

Kalland, Earl S. *Deuteronomy*. Vol. 3 of *The Expositors Bible Commentary*. Grand Rapids: Zondervan, 1992.

Kaplan, Louise J. *Adolescence: The Farewell to Childhood*. London: Jason Aronson, 1986.

Keck, Leander E. *1 Corinthians*. Vol. 10 of *The New Interpreter's Bible: A Commentary in Twelve Volumes*. Nashville: Abingdon, 2002.

Ketcham, Sharon Galgay. "Solving the Retention Problem Through Integration: A Communal Vision for Youth Ministry." *Journal of Youth Ministry* 11, no. 1 (2012).

Kirkwood, L. "An Artist's Perspective on Body Image, the Media, and Contemporary Society." *Journal of Nutrition, Education and Behavior* 37, Supplement 2 (November 2005): S125–32.

Kirn, Walter. "Will Teenagers Disappear?" *Time* (February 21, 2000), 60–61.

Kunkel, Dale. "Children and Television Advertising." *Handbook of Children and the Media*. Edited by Dorothy G. Singer and Jerome L. Singer. Thousand Oaks, CA: Sage, 2001.

Lamport, M. A. "Advancing the Field of Youth Ministry." *Christian Education Journal* 14, no. 3 (1996): 7–9.

———. "The State of the Profession of Youth Ministry." *Christian Education Journal* 13, no. 1 (1992): 85–100.

Larson, Reed. "Positive Youth Development, Willful Adolescents, and Mentoring." *Journal of Community Psychology* 34 no. 6 (2006): 678–79.

Lawson, Kevin E. "The Current State of the Educational Ministry Profession Part One: Perspective from the Frontlines." *Christian Education Journal* 15, no. 1 (1995): 9–27.

———. "The State of the Educational Ministry Profession in Evangelical Churches, Part 3: Advice for Future Staff and the Schools that Prepare Them." *Christian Education Journal* 16, no. 3 (1996): 95–109.

Leith, John H. *Crisis in the Church: The Plight of Theological Education.* Louisville, KY: John Knox, 1997.

Lindholm, Jennifer A. "The 'Interior' Lives of American College Students: Preliminary Findings from a National Study." *Passing on the Faith.* Edited by James L. Heft. New York: Fordham University Press, 2006.

Littleton, Jeanette Gardner. "Joining the Mission of Jesus: Interview with Ed Stetzer." *Grace and Peace* Magazine 18 (Fall 2018).

Livermore, David. "The Youth Ministry Education Debate: Irrelevant Theorists vs. Mindless Practitioners." *Journal of Youth Ministry* 1, no. 1 (2002): 89–102.

Loder, James E. *The Logic of the Spirit: Human Development in Theological Perspective.* San Francisco: Jossey-Bass, 1998.

Lynn, Robert, and Elliot Wright. *The Big Little School.* Birmingham, AL: Religious Education Press, 1971.

Maas, Robin, and Gabriel O'Donnel. *Spiritual Traditions for the Contemporary Church.* Nashville: Abingdon, 1990.

Maddix, Mark. "Christian Nurture and Conversion: A Conversation between Horace Bushnell and John Wesley." *Christian Education Journal* 9, no. 2 (2012): 311.

Mahler, Margaret S. *The Psychological Birth of the Human Infant.* New York: Basic Books, 2000.

Manual, Church of the Nazarene 2017-2021. Kansas City, MO: Nazarene Publishing House, 2017.

Mare, Harold W. *1 Corinthians.* Vol. 10 of *The Expositors Bible Commentary.* Grand Rapids: Zondervan, 1976.

Marqardt, Elizabeth. *Between Two Worlds: The Inner Lives of Children of Divorce.* New York: Crown, 2005.

Mason, Michael, Ivan Cheung, and Leslie Walker. "Substance Use, Social Networks, and the Geography of Urban Adolescents." *Substance Use and Misuse* 39, no. 10–12 (2004): 1751–77.

Masten, Ann S., Jelena Obradovic, and Keith B. Burt. "Resilience in Emerging Adulthood: Developmental Perspectives on Continuity and Transformation." *Emerging Adults in America: Coming of Age in the 21st Century.* Edited by Jeffrey Jensen Arnett and Jennifer Lynn Tanner. Washington, DC: American Psychological Association, 2006.

May, Rollo. *The Cry for Myth.* New York: Norton, 1991.

McGrath, Alister E. *Christian Spirituality: An Introduction.* Malden, MA: Blackwell Publishing, 1999.

Merton, Thomas. *Spiritual Direction and Meditation.* Collegeville, MN: Liturgical Press, 1960.

Milburn, Tim. *Leadership Starts with You.* Nampa, ID: Self-published, 2012.

Miller, Patrick D. *Deuteronomy; Interpretation: A Bible Commentary for Teaching and Preaching.* Louisville, KY: John Knox, 1990.

Nouwen, Henri J. M. *Life of the Beloved.* New York: Crossroad, 1992.

Noyce, Gaylord. *Pastoral Ethics: Professional Responsibilities of the Clergy.* Nashville: Parthenon Press, 1988.

Oden, Thomas C. *Pastoral Theology: Essentials of Ministry.* San Francisco: HarperCollins, 1983.

Oord, Thomas Jay, and Michael Lodahl. *Relational Holiness: Responding to the Call of Love.* Kansas City: Beacon Hill Press of Kansas City, 2005.

Outler, Albert C., ed. *John Wesley.* New York: Oxford, 1964.

Parks, Sharon Daloz. *Big Questions, Worthy Dreams: Mentoring Young Adults in Their Search for Meaning, Purpose, and Faith.* San Francisco: Jossey-Bass, 2000.

Paul, Jon. *Youth Ministry in Modern America: 1930 to the Present.* Grand Rapids: Baker Academic, 2000.

Pennebaker, James W., and Janel D. Seagal. "Forming a Story: The Health Benefits of Narrative." *Journal of Clinical Psychology* 55, no. 10 (Oct 1999): 1243–54.

Perry, W. *Forms of Intellectual and Ethical Development in the College Years.* New York: Holt, Rinehart and Winston, 1970.

Peterson, Brent D. *Created to Worship: God's Invitation to Become Fully Human.* Kansas City: Beacon Hill Press of Kansas City, 2012.

Piaget, Jean. *Judgment and Reasoning in the Child.* New York: Harcourt, Brace, 1928.

Plantinga, Cornelius. *Not the Way It's Supposed to Be: A Breviary of Sin.* Grand Rapids: Eerdmans, 1995.

Powell, Kara, Brad Griffin, and Cheryl Crawford. *Sticky Faith: Practical Ideas to Nurture Long-Term Faith in Teenagers.* Grand Rapids: Zondervan, 2011.

Powell, Kara, Jake Mulder, and Brad Griffin. *Growing Young: Six Essential Strategies to Help Young People Discover and Love Your Church.* Grand Rapids: Baker Books, 2016.

Putnam, Robert D. *Bowling Alone: The Collapse and Revival of American Community*. New York: Simon and Schuster, 2000.

Rahn, D. D. "What Kind of Education Do Youth Ministers Need?" *Christian Education Journal* 16, no. 3 (1996): 81–89.

Rappapport, L. *Personality Development*. Glenview, IL: Scott Foresman, 1972.

Rausch, Thomas P. "Where Do We Go from Here?" *America* 191, no. 11 (2004): 12–15.

Raymore, G. Godbey, and D. Crawford. "Self-Esteem, Gender and Socio-Economic Status: Their Relation to Perception of Constraint on Leisure Among Adolescents." *Journal of Leisure Research* 26 (1994): 99–118.

Reed, James E., and Ronnie Prevost. *A History of Christian Education*. Nashville: Broadman and Holman, 1993.

Richards, Lawrence O. *Youth Ministry: Its Renewal in the Local Church*. Grand Rapids: Zondervan, 1972.

Robbins, Duffy. *The Ministry of Nurture*. Grand Rapids: Zondervan, 1990.

Romanowski, William D. *Eyes Wide Open: Looking for God in Popular Culture*. Grand Rapids: Brazos, 2001.

Root, Andrew. *Revisiting Relational Youth Ministry: From a Strategy of Influence to a Theology of Incarnation*. Downers Grove, IL: InterVarsity, 2007.

———. *Taking the Cross to Youth Ministry: A Theological Journey through Youth Ministry*. Grand Rapids: Zondervan, 2012.

Santrock, John. *Adolescence*. 6th ed. Dubuque, IA: Brown and Benchmark, 1996.

Sawicki, Marianne. *The Gospel in History*. New York: Paulist Press, 1998.

Senter, Mark. *The Coming Revolution in Youth Ministry: And Its Radical Impact on the Church*. Wheaton, IL: Victor Books, 1992.

———. "History of Youth Ministry Education." *Christian Education Journal* 12, no. 2 (2014): 87.

———. "Moving Forward: A Perspective from the Chair of the AYME Board." *Journal of Youth Ministry* 6, no. 2 (SP 2008): 9–10.

———. *When God Shows Up: A History of Protestant Youth Ministry in America*. Grand Rapids: Baker Academic, 2010.

Severe, Michael K. "The Pac-Man Sydrome: The Missing Congruence of Philosophy and Practice in Youth Ministry." *Journal of Youth Ministry* 4, no. 2 (2006): 75–104.

Shelley, Bruce. "The Rise of Evangelical Youth Movements." *Fides et Historia* 18, no. 1 (1986).

Smith, Christian, and Melinda Lundquist Denton. *Soul Searching: The Religious and Spiritual Lives of American Teenagers*. Oxford: Oxford University Press, 2005.

Smith, Gordon T. *Called to Be Saints: An Invitation to Christian Maturity*. Downers Grove, IL: InterVarsity Press, 2014.

Smith, James K. A. *Imagining the Kingdom: How Worship Works*. Grand Rapids: Baker Academic, 2013.

———. *You Are What You Love: The Spiritual Power of Habit*. Grand Rapids: Brazos Press, 2016.

Stanley, Paul D., and J. Robert Clinton. *Connecting: The Mentoring Relationships You Need to Suceed in Life*. Colorado Springs, CO: NavPress, 1992.

Stone, Elizabeth. *Black Sheep and Kissing Cousins: How Our Family Stories Shape Us*. New York: Times Books, 1988.

Stott, John. *Christian Mission in the Modern World*. Downers Grove, IL: InterVarsity, via M. J. Murdock Charitable Trust, 2010.

———. "Mission: Rethinking Vocation." Vancouver, WA: Murdock Charitable Trust, 2012.

Strommen, Merton P. and Dick Hardel, eds. *Passing on the Faith: A Radical Model for Youth and Family Ministry, Revised*. Winona, MN: Saint Mary's Press, 2008.

Strommen, Merton P., Karen E. Jones, and Dave Rahn. *Youth Ministry That Transforms: A Comprehensive Analysis of the Hopes, Frustrations, and Effectiveness of Today's Youth Workers*. Grand Rapids: Zondervan, 2001.

Tigay, Jeffery H., ed. *Deuteronomy: The JPS Commentary*. Philadelphia: Jewish Publication Society, 1996.

Twenge, Jean M. *Generation Me: Why Today's Young Americans Are More Confident, Assertive, Entitled—and More Miserable than Ever Before*. New York: Free Press, 2006.

Tyson, John R., ed. *Invitation to Christian Spirituality: An Ecumenical Anthology*. New York: Oxford University Press, 1999.

Willard, Dallas. *The Spirit of the Disciplines: Understanding How God Changes Lives*. New York: Harper Collins Publishers, 1988.

Wilson, Jonathan R. *God's Good World: Reclaiming the Doctrine of Creation*. Grand Rapids: Baker Academic, 2013.

Wolff, Leanne O. "Family Narrative: How Our Stories Shape Us." *Annual Meeting of the Speech Communication Association* 1–20. Miami Beach, 1993.

Wright, Christopher J. H. *The Mission of God: Unlocking the Bible's Grand Narrative*. Downer's Grove, IL: InterVarsity Press, 2006.

Wright, N. T. *After You Believe: Why Christian Character Matters*. New York: HarperOne, 2010.

———. *Simply Christian: Why Christianity Makes Sense*. New York: HarperOne, 2006.

————. *Surprised by Hope: Rethinking Heaven, the Resurrection, and the Mission of the Church.* 1st ed. New York: HarperOne, 2008.

Wright, Walter C. *Mentoring: The Promise of Relational Leadership.* Waynesboro, GA: Paternoster Press, 2006.

Notes

● ● ● ● ● ● ● ● ● ● ● ● ●

Introduction

1. Kenda Creasy Dean, Chap Clark, and Dave Rahn, eds., *Starting Right: Thinking Theologically about Youth Ministry* (Grand Rapids: Zondervan, 2001), 45–46.

2. Jeffrey Jensen Arnett, *Emerging Adulthood: The Winding Road from the Late Teens through the Twenties* (New York: Oxford, 2004), 102–3.

3. Kara E. Powell, Brad M. Griffin, Cheryl A. Crawford, *Sticky Faith: Practical Ideas to Nurture Long-Term Faith in Teenagers* (Grand Rapids: Zondervan, 2011), 15.

4. Ray S. Anderson, *The Soul of Ministry: Forming Leaders for God's People* (Louisville, KY: Westminster John Knox, 1997), 26.

5. Ibid.

6. Ibid.

7. Ray S. Anderson, *The Shape of Practical Theology: Empowering Ministry with Theological Praxis* (Downers Grove, IL: InterVarsity Press, 2001), 49–50.

8. Donald A. Hagner, *Matthew*, vols. 33A and 33B in *Word Biblical Commentary* (Dallas: Word, 1993), 135.

9. Ibid., 136.

10. Thomas Jay Oord and Michael Lodahl, *Relational Holiness: Responding to the Call of Love* (Kansas City: Beacon Hill Press of Kansas City, 2005), 60–61.

11. Duffy Robbins, *The Ministry of Nurture* (Grand Rapids: Zondervan, 1990), 17.

12. See James K. A. Smith, *You Are What You Love: The Spiritual Power of Habit* (Grand Rapids: Brazos, 2016).

13. Kevin Lambert, blog post in response to a blog of a UMC pastor who left the Church of the Nazarene. Used with permission.

Chapter 1

1. http://www.merriam-webster.com/dictionary/integration (accessed May 28, 2013).

2. Sharon Galgay Ketcham, "Solving the Retention Problem Through Integration: A Communal Vision for Youth Ministry," *Journal of Youth Ministry* 11, no. 1 (2012): 10.

3. It is interesting to note the characterization of an "ear" both here and in the oft-quoted article of Stuart Cummings-Bond, "The One-Eared Mickey Mouse," published in *Youthworker* (Fall 1989).

4. Additionally, Paul's advice to Timothy (1 Timothy 4:12) is a helpful reminder: "Don't let anyone look down on you because you are young, but set an example for the believers in speech, in conduct, in love, in faith and in purity."

5. Richard B. Hays, *First Corinthians; Interpretation: A Bible Commentary for Teaching and Preaching* (Louisville, KY: John Knox, 1997), 215.

6. This does not even begin to address those with disabilities or special needs or who are marginalized for a multitude of reasons.

7. Christian Smith, "Let's Stop 'Student' Talk in Youth Ministry," *Youth Worker Journal* 25, no. 2 (2008): 96.

8. Andrew Root, "Stop Calling Them Students," *Immerse Journal* (November/ December 2012), 21–25.

9. Ibid., 24.

10. Ibid.

11. *Anchor Bible Dictionary* (New York: Doubleday 1992), 1:770.

12. Commission on Children at Risk, Institute for American Values, "Hardwired to Connect: The New Scientific Case for Authoritative Communities" (2003).

13. Ibid., 52.

14. http://www.ymresourcer.com/model/misstat.htm (accessed June 17, 2014).

15. Ibid.

16. http://www.riverroadchurchofchrist.com/youth_ministry (accessed June 17, 2014).

17. Fuller Youth Institute (FYI) pins this number to be between forty and sixty percent. For more on FYI, see www.fulleryouthinstitute.org and www.stickyfaith.org.

18. Andrew Root, *Revisiting Relational Youth Ministry: From a Strategy of Influence to a Theology of Incarnation* (Downers Grove, IL: InterVarsity, 2007).

19. Christian Smith and Melinda Lundquist Denton, *Soul Searching: The Religious and Spiritual Lives of American Teenagers* (Oxford: Oxford University Press, 2005), as found in Ketcham, "Solving the Retention Problem Through Integration."

20. Root, *Revisiting Relational Youth Ministry*, 208.

21. Powell, Griffin, and Crawford, *Sticky Faith*.

22. Darrell L. Guder, ed., *Missional Church: A Vision for the Sending of the Church in North America* (Grand Rapids: Eerdmans, 1998).

23. J. G. Davies, *Worship and Mission* (1966), 28, as quoted in John Stott, *Christian Mission in the Modern World* (Downers Grove, IL: InterVarsity, via M. J. Murdock Charitable Trust, 2010), 10.

24. http://www.merriam-webster.com/dictionary/centrifugal (accessed June 19, 2014).

25. N. T. Wright, *Simply Christian: Why Christianity Makes Sense* (New York: HarperOne, 2006), xi.

26. Timothy Paul Jones, ed., *Perspectives on Family Ministry: Three Views* (Nashville: B&H Academic, 2009).

27. Ibid., 147.

28. Ibid.

29. Kenda Creasy Dean, *Almost Christian: What the Faith of Our Teenagers Is Telling the American Church* (New York: Oxford, 2010), 5.

30. Ideas in this section come from John Stott's wonderful little book titled *Mission: Rethinking Vocation*, which was printed with permission by the Murdock Family Trust in 2012.

31. Stott, *Mission: Rethinking Vocation*, 25–26 (emphasis mine).

32. Jeffrey Jensen Arnett, *Emerging Adulthood: The Winding Road from the Late Teens through the Twenties* (New York: Oxford 2004), 140.

33. R. Joiner, "Clearing Up Family Ministry Confusion" (www.orangeleaders.com), as reported in Jones, *Perspectives on Family Ministry*, 149.

Chapter 2

1. After serving for eighteen years at CCN, Johnny is now the lead pastor at Tree City Church of the Nazarene in Boise, Idaho.

2. That phrase "Organize to the Win" is one I learned from reading Andy Stanley's book *Seven Principles of Effective Leadership*, but it is not unique to him—it is a common language used in business leadership.

Section II

1. Ron King as quoted in DeVries, *Sustainable Youth Ministry*, 13.

2. As reported in DeVries, *Sustainable Youth Ministry*, 11.

3. Jonathan Grenz, "Factors Influencing Vocational Changes Among Youth Ministers," *Journal of Youth Ministry* 1, no. 1 (Fall 2002).

4. As reported in Tim Milburn, *Leadership Starts with You* (self-published, 2012).

Chapter 3

1. *Church of the Nazarene Manual* 2017–2021 (Kansas City: Nazarene Publishing House, 2017), paragraphs 159–159.3.

2. Can find at: http://store.churchlawtodaystore.com/20cohaforchs1.html.

3. Chart found in link to Twitter @ronlieber sent on May 18, 2017, at 8:43 a.m. on www.cnbc.com, "NerdWallet Chart Shows the Power of Compound Interest, 2017/09/27."

4. www.psychologytoday.com/us/blog/feeling-it/201708/three-science-based-reasons-vacation-boosts-productivity, and www.nypost.com/2018/07/23/proof-that-a-four-day-work-week-makes-us-better-employees/ (accessed November 14, 2018).

5. For questions to ask in an interview see: www.topresume.com or www.glassdoor.com, "8 Questions to Ask in an Interview." Some additional questions are: What is the purpose of youth ministry? How will you determine if I am doing my job? How will I be evaluated each year? What is the metric for "effectiveness"? How long do you

plan to be the lead pastor of this church? How is budgeting decided upon? What are your goals for one, three, five, and ten years here? What is the strategy to meet those goals?

6. Joe Gorman, *Healthy. Happy. Holy.: 7 Practices Toward a Holistic Life* (Kansas City: The Foundry Publishing, 2018), 18 (emphasis mine).

7. Mark Hayse, *Youth Ministry, Obesity, and the Rhetorics of Faith*, unpublished paper presented at the 2012 Association of Youth Ministry Educators Conference, Dallas, TX, October 2012.

8. A terrific resource for youth workers seeking advice on the entire job search process from searching to interviewing to landing is *The Indispensable Youth Pastor: Land, Love, and Lock in Your Youth Ministry Dream Job*, by Mark DeVries and Jeff Dunn-Rankin.

9. www.youthleader.net.

10. A condition of feeling disappointed that Sunday didn't go as well as you'd hoped, planned, or anticipated . . . or maybe you got hijacked by an unhappy congregant. Or you know it's when the day just kind of stinks.

11. Brent D. Peterson, *Created to Worship: God's Invitation to Become Fully Human* (Kansas City: Beacon Hill Press of Kansas City, 2012), 42.

12. Thanks to a beloved mentor of mine, the late Brennan Manning, for so often preaching this to me through his books and in person.

Section III

1. https://proto-knowledge.blogspot.com/2010/11/what-is-wrong-with-young -people-today.html (accessed October 24, 2018).

2. https://www.ranker.com/list/notable-and-famous-youth-quotes/reference (accessed October 24, 2018).

Chapter 4

1. G. Stanley Hall, *Adolescence: Its Psychology and Its Relations to Physiology, Anthropology, Sociology, Sex, Crime, Religion and Education* (New York: D. Appleton and Co., 1904), xiii.

2. Dean, Clark, and Rahn, *Starting Right*, 44.

3. Margaret S. Mahler, *The Psychological Birth of the Human Infant* (New York: Basic Books, 2000), 3–4.

4. Peter Blos, *The Adolescent Passage: Developmental Issues* (New York: International Universities Press, 1979), 142.

5. John Santrock, *Adolescence*, 6th ed. (Dubuque, Iowa: Brown and Benchmark, 1996), 87.

6. http://www.ncbi.nlm.nih.gov/pubmed/12509562 (accessed May 28, 2015).

7. Dean, Clark, and Rahn, *Starting Right*, 46.

8. Ibid., 50.

9. Jeffrey Jensen Arnett, *Readings on Adolescence and Emerging Adulthood* (Upper Saddle River, NJ: Prentice Hall, 2002), 25–26.

10. Jean Piaget, *Judgment and Reasoning in the Child* (New York: Harcourt, Brace and Company, 1928).

11. Erik H. Erikson, *Identity and Life Cycle* (New York: W. W. Norton and Co., 1980), 50.

12. Erik H. Erikson, *Identity: Youth and Crisis* (New York: W. W. Norton and Co., 1968), 91–92.

13. Carl G. Jung, *Personality Types* (Princeton, NJ: Princeton University Press, 1971), 448.

14. James E. Loder, *Logic of the Spirit: Human Development in Theological Perspective* (San Francisco: John Wiley and Sons, Inc., 1998), 286.

15. As summarized by Chap Clark. See Dean, Clark, and Rahn, *Starting Right*, 54.

16. For more on the nature vs. nurture debate, see Stephen J. Ceci and Wendy M. Williams, eds., *The Nature-Nurture Debate: The Essential Readings* (Malden, MA: Blackwell Publishers Ltd., 1999).

17. Urie Bronfenbrenner, *The Ecology of Human Development: Experiments by Nature and Design* (Cambridge, MA: Harvard University Press, 1979), 16–17.

18. James Gollnick, *Religion and Spirituality in the Life Cycle* (New York: Peter Lang Publishing, 2005), 100.

19. Ronald E. Dahl and Linda Patia Spear, eds., *Adolescent Brain Development: Vulnerabilities and Opportunities* (New York: The New York Academy of Sciences, 2004), 311–12.

20. David Alan Black, *The Myth of Adolescence: Raising Responsible Children in an Irresponsible Society* (Yorba Linda, CA: Davidson Press, 1999).

21. Robert Epstein, *The Case Against Adolescence: Rediscovering the Adult in Every Teen* (Fresno, CA: Quill Driver Books, 2007), 5.

22. Ibid., 9.

23. U.S. Department of Health and Human Services, "Positive Youth Development," http://www.acf.hhs.gov/programs/fysb/content/positiveyouth/index.htm (accessed May 13, 2009).

24. Reed Larson, "Positive Youth Development, Willful Adolescents, and Mentoring," *Journal of Community Psychology* 34, no. 6 (2006): 678–79.

25. David Elkind, *The Hurried Child, 25th Anniversary Ed.* (Cambridge, MA: Perseus Books, 2007), 172.

26. Archibald D. Hart, *Adrenaline and Stress* (Nashville: Thomas Nelson, 1995), 37.

27. Elkind, *The Hurried Child*, 134.

28. Chap Clark, *Hurt: Inside the World of Today's Teenagers* (Grand Rapids: Baker Academic, 2004), 55 and 60.

29. Megan Howard and Jon Barrett, ed., *Teen People Faith: Stories of Belief and Spirituality* (New York: Harper Collins Publishers, 2001), xi.

30. Alister E. McGrath, *Christian Spirituality: An Introduction* (Malden, MA: Blackwell Publishing, 1999), 2.

31. John R. Tyson, ed., *Invitation to Christian Spirituality: An Ecumenical Anthology* (New York: Oxford University Press, 1999), 1.

32. Dallas Willard, *The Spirit of the Disciplines: Understanding How God Changes Lives* (New York: Harper Collins Publishers, 1988), ix.

33. John Drane, *Do Christians Know How to Be Spiritual?: The Rise of New Spirituality and the Mission of the Church* (London: Darton, Longman, and Todd, Ltd., 2005), 41.

34. David Augsburger, *Dissident Discipleship: A Spirituality of Self-Surrender, Love of God, and Love of Neighbor* (Grand Rapids: Brazos Press, 2006), 7–12.

Chapter 5

1. http://owic.oregonstate.edu/california-black-oak-quercus-kelloggii (accessed September 19, 2018).

2. Owic.oregonstate.edu.

3. Doug Fields, *Purpose-Driven Youth Ministry: 9 Essential Foundations for Healthy Growth* (Grand Rapids: Zondervan, 1998).

4. Be sure to read the chapter on evangelism by Tom Combes, at the end of this book. I'm not sure we do "evangelism" very well anymore. So much has changed and we are stuck in old methodologies. Tom is a southeastern U.S. division leader in Young Life. Tom provides not only a helpful reframing of the importance of but also a solid philosophical approach to evangelism/outreach.

Section IV

1. Christian Smith and Melinda Lundquist Denton, *Soul Searching: The Religious and Spiritual Loves of American Teenagers* (New York: Oxford, 2005), 261.

2. Kenda Dean as quoted by Mark DeVries, *Sustainable Youth Ministry: Why Most Youth Ministry Doesn't Last and What Your Church Can Do about It* (Downers Grove, IL: InterVarsity, 2008), 142.

3. Kenda Dean and Ron Foster, *The Godbearing Life: The Art of Soul Tending for Youth Ministry* (Nashville: Upper Room, 1998), 99.

4. Sharon Galgay Ketcham, "Solving the Retention Problem Through Integration: A Communal Vision for Youth Ministry," *Journal of Youth Ministry* 26.

Chapter 6

1. Dean and Foster, *The Godbearing Life*, 36.

2. Root, *Revisiting Relational Youth Ministry*, 201.

3. Ibid.

4. DeVries, *Sustainable Youth Ministry*, 61.

5. Wesley Black as quoted in Ketcham, "Solving the Retention Problem Through Integration," 9.

6. A great app is YouthTracker: www.youthgrouptracker.com.

7. Kara Powell, Jake Mulder, and Brad Griffin, *Growing Young: Six Essential Strategies to Help Young People Discover and Love Your Church* (Grand Rapids: Baker Books, 2016), 196.

8. Ibid.

9. Ibid., 208.

10. Kenda Dean, *Almost Christian: What the Faith of Our Teenagers Is Telling the American Church* (New York: Oxford, 2010), 24.

11. Dean and Foster, *The Godbearing Life*, 72.

12. See the helpful book by Powell, Griffin, and Crawford, *Sticky Faith*.

13. See Appendix A and Appendix B for examples of a Sunday School Exchange meeting outline.

14. Smith and Denton as quoted by Ketcham, "Solving the Retention Problem Through Integration," 9.

15. Joiner, "Clearing Up Family Ministry Confusion" (www.orangeleaders.com), as reported in *Perspectives on Family Ministry*, 149.

16. As reported in Dean, *Almost Christian*, 18.

17. Merton P. Strommen and Dick Hardel, eds., *Passing on the Faith: A Radical Model for Youth and Family Ministry, Revised* (Winona, MN: Saint Mary's Press, 2008), 41.

18. Ibid.

19. DeVries, *Sustainable Youth Ministry*, 60.

20. Visit www.commonsensemedia.com to discover the wealth of resources available for parents, educators, and young people.

21. Fields, *Purpose-Driven Youth Ministry*, 252.

22. Here are just three: 1997 Adolescent Health Study as reported in Thomas Hine, *The Rise and Fall of the American Teenager*; Smith and Denton, *Soul Searching: The Religious and Spiritual Lives of American Teenagers*, 267; Powell, Griffin, and Crawford, *Sticky Faith: Practical Ideas to Nurture Long-Term Faith in Teenagers*.

23. Smith and Denton, *Soul Searching*, 267.

24. Ibid.

25. The author heard this phrase from Dr. Cormode numerous times in the Sticky Faith Cohort visits he made to Fuller Theological Seminary in 2012-13.

26. Although this book was written over twenty years ago, it is an excellent resource and provides an extremely helpful way of structuring and addressing the various aspects of church-based youth ministry.

27. For more on "place-sharing," see Andrew Root's excellent book, *Revisiting Relational Youth Ministry*.

Section V

1. "Joining the Mission of Jesus: An Interview with Ed Stetzer," interview with Jeanette Gardner Littleton in *Grace and Peace Magazine*, Issue 18 (Fall 2018): 46.

2. Keith Drury, *The Call of a Lifetime* (Indianapolis: Wesleyan, 2013), 29.

3. Dean and Foster, *The Godbearing Life*, 9.

4. Ibid., 36.

Chapter 7

1. "Joining the Mission of Jesus," 48.

2. Smith and Denton, *Soul Searching*, 163.

3. Ibid., 162–63.

4. Dean, *Almost Christian*, 37 (emphasis mine).

5. Milburn, *Leadership Starts with You*, 21.

6. Gorman, *Happy. Healthy. Holy.*, 15.

7. When I say, "affirmation, acceptance, and love for all" I do not mean—in any way—to affirm or accept or love a sinful lifestyle or choice. I do mean to affirm each person's humanity and the fact that each person carries the *imago Dei*—image of God—in their being. I mean to accept them as they are but to love them enough to encourage them to grow up into Christ and leave the past behind and strain toward the upward call for which "God has called [them] heavenward in Jesus Christ" (Philippians 3:14).

8. Smith, *You Are What You Love*, 29.

9. Dean, *Almost Christian*, 41.

10. Ibid., 42.

11. Thanks to my friend and colleague Joe Gorman for making this point to me.

Chapter 8

1. Chap Clark, *Hurt 2.0: Inside the World of Today's Teenagers* (Grand Rapids: Baker Academic, 2011), 169.

2. James E. Loder, *The Logic of the Spirit: Human Development in Theological Perspective* (San Francisco: Jossey-Bass Publishers, 1998), 203–4.

3. Andrew Root, *Taking the Cross to Youth Ministry: A Theological Journey through Youth Ministry* (Grand Rapids: Zondervan, 2012), 51.

4. See Christopher J. H. Wright, *The Mission of God: Unlocking the Bible's Grand Narrative* (Downers Grove, IL: InterVarsity Press, 2006), 155.

5. Cornelius Plantinga, *Not the Way It's Supposed to Be: A Breviary of Sin* (Grand Rapids: Eerdmans, 1995), 5.

6. Jonathan R. Wilson, *God's Good World: Reclaiming the Doctrine of Creation* (Grand Rapids: Baker Academic, 2013), 79–81.

7. N. T. Wright, *After You Believe: Why Christian Character Matters* (New York: HarperOne, 2010), 219.

8. Anderson, *The Shape of Practical Theology*, 109. Anderson believed that, in order to take into account the influence of history, tradition, and preference in ministry, there must be biblical antecedents for every case of eschatological preference to properly shape and orient ministry praxis.

9. "Technology is the knack for so arranging the world that we do not experience it" (Rollo May, *The Cry for Myth* [New York: Norton, 1991], 57).

10. Douglas John Hall, *Professing the Faith: Christian Theology in a North American Context* (Minneapolis: Fortress Press, 1996), 305–6.

11. James K. A. Smith, *Imagining the Kingdom: How Worship Works* (Grand Rapids: Baker Academic, 2013), 12–13.

12. Ibid., 2.

13. N. T. Wright, *Surprised by Hope: Rethinking Heaven, the Resurrection, and the Mission of the Church* (New York: HarperOne, 2008), 95.

14. Paul King Jewett and Marguerite Shuster, *Who We Are: Our Dignity as Human; A Neo-Evangelical Theology* (Grand Rapids: Eerdmans, 1996), 29.

15. Walter Brueggemann, *Genesis: Interpretation: A Bible Commentary for Teaching and Preaching* (Louisville: Westminster John Knox Press, 1982), 32.

16. To be clear, this is not dignity as it is understood as a modern concept, whereas, "To treat humans according to their dignity is to treat them as if they owned themselves and had a right to determine their own actions. . . . A being's dignity increases or declines with their level of independence. The more self-sufficient and self-defining we are, the more dignity we have" (Ron Highfield, *God, Freedom and Human Dignity: Embracing a God-Centered Identity in a Me-Centered Culture* [Downers Grove, IL: InterVarsity Press, 2013], 96).

17. Hemchand Gossai, "Divine Evaluation and the Quest for a Suitable Companion," *Cross Currents* 52 (Winter 2004): 546.

18. Highfield, *God, Freedom and Human Dignity*, 126.

19. Dean, Clark, and Rahn, *Starting Right*, 111.

20. Gordon T. Smith, *Called to Be Saints: An Invitation to Christian Maturity* (Downers Grove, IL: InterVarsity Press, 2014), 133.

21. Peter L. Berger and Thomas Luckmann, *The Social Construction of Reality: A Treatise in the Sociology of Knowledge* (Garden City, NY: Doubleday, 1966), 102.

22. Chap Clark, "The Adoption View of Youth Ministry," in *Youth Ministry in the 21st Century* (Grand Rapids: Baker Academic, 2015), 85.

23. George Hunter III, *The Celtic Way of Evangelism: How Christianity Can Reach the West . . . Again* (Nashville: Abingdon Press, 2000), 99–100.

24. Anderson, *The Shape of Practical Theology*, 240.

Excursus

1. See James E. Reed and Ronnie Prevost, *A History of Christian Education* (Nashville: Broadman and Holman, 1993), and James Riley Estep, Jonathan Hyung-

soo Kim, Alvin Wallace Kuest, and Mark Amos Maddix, C.E.: The Heritage of Christian Education (Joplin, MO: College Press, 2003).

2. Dean Blevins and Mark A. Maddix, Discovering Discipleship: Dynamics of Christian Education (Kansas City: Beacon Hill Press of Kansas City, 2010), 43.

3. Estep et al., C.E.: The Heritage of Christian Education, 2.2.

4. Ibid., 4.16.

5. Blevins and Maddix, Discovering Discipleship, 45.

6. Ibid., 46.

7. Marianne Sawicki, The Gospel in History (New York: Paulist Press, 1998), 112.

8. Reed and Prevost, A History of Christian Education, 111–19.

9. Mark W. Cannister, "Youth Ministry's Historical Context: The Education and Evangelism of Young People," in Dean, Clark, and Rahn, Starting Right, 78.

10. Blevins and Maddix, Discovering Discipleship, 47–48.

11. Ibid., 48.

12. Ibid., 49.

13. Reed and Prevost, A History of Christian Education, 255–58.

14. Mark Senter III, "History of Youth Ministry Education," in Christian Education Journal 12, no. 2 (2014): 87.

15. Robert Lynn and Elliot Wright, The Big Little School (Birmingham, AL: Religious Education Press, 1971), 56.

16. Senter, "History of Youth Ministry Education," 88.

17. Mark Senter III, When God Shows Up: A History of Protestant Youth Ministry in America (Grand Rapids: Baker Academic, 2010), 109–11.

18. Mark Maddix, "Christian Nurture and Conversion: A Conversation between Horace Bushnell and John Wesley," in Christian Education Journal 9, no. 2 (2012): 311. For a further biographical history of Horace Bushnell, see Robert B. Mullins, The Puritan as Yankee: The Life of Horace Bushnell (Grand Rapids: Eerdmans, 2002).

19. Maddix, "Christian Nurture and Conversion," 311.

20. Horace Bushnell, Christian Nurture (New York: Charles Scribner, 1961), 10.

21. Perry Downs, "Christian Nurture: A Comparison of Horace Bushnell and Lawrence O. Richards," in Christian Education Journal 4, no. 2 (1983): 44.

22. Cannister, "Youth Ministry's Historical Context," 81.

23. Ibid., 82.

24. Ibid., 83.

25. Senter, When God Shows Up, 59.

26. Ibid.

27. Ibid.

28. See Kenda Creasy Dean, Practicing Passion: Youth and the Quest for a Passionate Church (Grand Rapids: Eerdmans, 2004).

29. Senter, When God Shows Up, 84.

30. For further discussion about four youth ministry movements that had the most significant impact on the second half of the twentieth century, see Jon Paul, *Youth Ministry in Modern America: 1930 to the Present* (Grand Rapids: Baker Academic, 2000). These youth movements include the Walther Youth League (Lutheran), Young Christian Works (Roman Catholic), Youth for Christ (Evangelical Protestant), and African American congregational youth ministry (Methodist, Baptist, and United Church of Christ).

31. Bruce Shelley, "The Rise of Evangelical Youth Movements," in *Fides et Historia* 18, no. 1 (1986): 49.

32. Ibid., 50.

33. Cannister, "Youth Ministry's Historical Context," 87.

34. Senter, *When God Shows Up,* 74.

35. Shelley, "The Rise of Evangelical Youth Movements," 52.

36. Cannister, "Youth Ministry's Historical Context," 89.

37. Shelley, "The Rise of Evangelical Youth Movements," 55.

38. http://www.intervarsity.org/about/our/history.

39. http://nazarene.org/ministries/ssm/children/programs/caravan/history/display.html.

40. http://youthspecialties.com/aboutus/ourstory/.

41. This does not mean that the social sciences are not important, but they should be evaluated through a theological lens.

42. Senter, "History of Youth Ministry Education," 102.

43. See Root, *Revisiting Relational* Youth Ministry.